Advance praise for

The Gospels According to St.

This book is filled with the Spirit and with the Gospel that were Spirit and life for St. Francis. Fr. Hilarion Kistner, himself a Scripture scholar and teacher, has drawn on a lifetime of scholarship and of living the Gospel to write a book for everyone, scholar and non-scholar, the churched and non-churched. It is a book about how St. Francis found the Spirit of God in God's words, and how St. Francis's own words in turn radiate that same Spirit of God calling us to live what we read here. This book can change your life.

—Murray Bodo, O.F.M.
author, *Francis: The Journey and the Dream*

Fr. Hilarion Kistner, O.F.M., uses his knowledge of Scripture to open up the way St. Francis of Assisi uses Scripture in his writings. He explores the foundational texts that moved St. Francis to begin his way of life, and the references to Scripture in his Rule, prayers, letters, and admonitions. Fr. Kistner's tone and style are pastoral and colloquial; as you read, you feel like you are having a conversation with him over a cup of coffee.

—Jeffrey Scheeler, O.F.M.
provincial minister, Province of St. John the Baptist

Great insight and wisdom comes with humility, experience, and knowledge. Fr. Kistner taps all three elements in writing this clear exposition of how St. Francis interpreted the Gospel texts, which were Francis's inspiration and compelled him to preach by example and his words. The five principles of Francis's way of interpreting the texts are adequately summarized in five words: literal, realistic, personal, practical and spiritual. I am delighted with *The Gospels According to St. Francis* and I heartily endorse it to all who are inspired by this great saint of Assisi.

—Dan Kroger, O.F.M.

publisher, Franciscan Media

Francis of Assisi saw the Gospels not as ideals to be admired from afar but something to be lived generously. This fine book shows how the word of God changed Francis and can change us.

—Pat McCloskey, O.F.M.

Franciscan editor for *St. Anthony Messenger*

Drawing on his love of Sacred Scripture and his love of St. Francis, Fr. Hilarion offers a simple, practical and effective way to dialogue with God through his Word. Following the Poor Man of Assisi, he guides us into a deeper, Spirit-driven life with the Gospel at its core. Fr. Hilarion does not give us *answers* but a *method* for opening the Scriptures and making them our own.

—Frank J. Jasper, O.F.M.

THE GOSPELS ACCORDING TO
SAINT FRANCIS

HILARION KISTNER, O.F.M.

Franciscan
MEDIA
Cincinnati, Ohio

Cover and book design by Mark Sullivan
Cover image: St. Francis receiving the stigmata, c.1580,
Germain Pilon. ©bridgemanart.com

Scripture passages have been taken from *New Revised Standard
Version Bible,* copyright ©1989 by the Division of Christian
Education of the National Council of the Churches of Christ in
the U.S.A., and used by permission. All rights reserved.
The author gratefully acknowledges the work of Knut Willem
Ruyter, O.F.M., for some of the ideas developed in this book,
especially "Bible Interpretation by Francis and His Followers:
Some Hermeneutical Principles" (parts one and two),
appearing in *The Cord: A Franciscan Spiritual Review,*
March and April, 1983.

LIBRARY OF CONGRESS CATALOGING-IN-PUBLICATION DATA
Kistner, Hilarion.
The gospels according to St. Francis / Hilarion Kistner.
pages cm
Includes bibliographical references.
ISBN 978-1-61636-728-2 (alk. paper)
1. Francis, of Assisi, Saint, 1182-1226. 2. Jesus Christ—Person
and offices. 3. Bible. Gospels—Criticism, interpretation, etc. I.
Title.
BX4700.F6K58 2014
271'.302—dc23
2013045197

ISBN 978-1-61636-728-2

Published by Franciscan Media
28 W. Liberty St.
Cincinnati, OH 45202
www.FranciscanMedia.org

Printed in the United States of America.
Printed on acid-free paper.
14 15 16 17 18 5 4 3 2 1

To the memory of
Ignatius Brady, O.F.M.,
(1911–1990)
who helped many to know and love
St. Francis.

CONTENTS

$\mathscr{H}$ow excited and honored I am to write a short foreword for the friar who first taught me Scripture! It was Fr. Hilarion, or "Hank" as we young ones sometimes called him, who for the four years following the opening of the Second Vatican Council (1966–1970), patiently, lovingly, and studiously introduced us to the scholars, the hermeneutics, and the texts that would change our lives. At least, he changed mine.

The Jerusalem Bible had just been published in 1966 with all of its excellent, up-to-date footnotes. That first edition, which I began to mark up in his class, is the one I have continued to use to this day. It has been rebound twice and traveled all over the world. It is filled with yellow highlighting, marginal notes, significant dates when it deeply spoke to me, short commentaries, and some question marks where I just don't get it! It has been "thumped" in many a pulpit! Some books, especially for some reason Genesis, Matthew, Luke, 1 and 2 Corinthians, are dirty and dog-eared from overuse. I have seriously asked the friars to bury it with me since I know it would be very helpful material for anyone seeking to inaugurate my posthumous heresy trial. No disinterment allowed!

I remember getting a paper returned from Fr. Hilarion where he rightly gave me a B- because I took off on my own idiosyncratic tangents on the theme of "the Son of Man" instead of showing that I understood the scholarship and the texts themselves. We young friars were reveling in the new freedom of the post-Vatican II era, which must have driven our doctoral professors crazy, but I never felt anything but kindness, and a few rolled eyes, from Fr. Hilarion.

Fortunately for all of us, Hank now gives St. Francis an A+! As he indeed should.

I was asked to write this at a perfect time because I have just finished a book of my own on the alternative vision of Francis for Franciscan Media, and this entire year of reading and studying Francis, Clare, Anthony, and Bonaventure, has surely revealed to me how deeply scriptural the early Franciscan movement was. If Francis's "literal, realistic, personal, practical, and spiritual" approach to Scripture (which Fr.

Hilarion so brilliantly summarizes in this book) had held sway in the Catholic world, I sincerely believe that much of the anger and criticism aimed at the Roman Church by the early Reformers would have been without foundation. I do not say that lightly. No wonder some have praised Francis as "the First Protestant." His genius was that he was able to do it from within by emphasizing lifestyle quotes instead of quotes that might question dogmas, doctrines, or authority. He preached with his life, just as Pope Francis is doing today.

I have often even said to ecumenical gatherings that St. Francis was in some ways a fundamentalist, but he was fundamentalist about those passages that asked a lot of himself and his "form of life," whereas most reformers (and preachers) are fundamentalist about passages that ask a lot of others, judge others, or condemn others. Francis, just as Paul advised, "taught spiritual things spiritually" (1 Corinthians 2:13). In him we find none of the rancor, fire and brimstone, or negativity that has characterized so many who have wanted in their own way to return us to our Gospel foundations. Francis just did it himself, and I believe that is his alternative orthodoxy. He just emphasized very different things, usually having to do with practice, prayer, and simplicity. Who could argue with that? Instead of fighting power, or vying for power, he ran to the Gospel place of powerlessness. And now we continue to run after him.

I remember being inspired when I asked Fr. Hilarion what he wrote his doctoral thesis on, and he told me it was on one line from St. Paul. I ran to my friendly Jerusalem Bible to look up 2 Corinthians 8:9 where it is still highlighted: "Remember how generous the Lord Jesus was: he was rich, but he became poor for your sake, to make you rich out of his poverty." My young mind could not imagine how you could do a whole thesis on such a small, simple phrase pulled out of St. Paul's letter.

Yet now, almost fifty years later I can only begin to realize what it says about Fr. Hilarion's own youthful spirituality, his early love of the Franciscan way, and his desire to pass it on to others.

As he did to me, and as he will now do for you.

So gratefully,
Richard Rohr, O.F.M.

ACKNOWLEDGMENTS

The many people who helped bring this book to completion are too numerous to name, but I would like to thank especially Mary Carol Kendzia and Katie Carroll, for their editorial expertise; Ron Cooper at the Franciscan Archives, for his patient help; my brother and sister Franciscans; and all the staff at Franciscan Media.

Robert Farrar Capon was an Episcopal priest, a theologian, a teacher, and author of over twenty books. One of those books, written in the late 1970s, is called *Hunting the Divine Fox*. The book is really an exercise in theology. Not many of us have ever experienced a fox hunt, but we have all seen pictures of them in a book or scenes in a movie.

One of the things Capon notes in his book is that it takes a while to find out where the fox is. It takes the dogs a while to get on track, to get the scent of the fox and go after it. And then, even after they do so, the fox manages frequently to disappear. Only once in a while do you catch a glimpse of the fox, maybe see him running along, trying to stay ahead of the dogs.

This is really a nice parable, or even an allegory, of what theology is about. It is also useful in showing something of what we are going to do in this book, as we examine the importance of Scripture in the life and teaching of St. Francis of Assisi.

Really, all of us are hunting the divine fox. We are all looking for God, whether we know it or not; that's true of those of us who actively participate in a religion or acknowledge our faith, as well as of all the people in the world who are seemingly indifferent to God. Deep down inside, all of us seek the divine source of our being.

And it's also true that all of us have a hard time getting a hold on this God. When we begin to look for him, it takes a while even to catch a glimpse of him. And even after we catch a glimpse of God we can never really capture him—but that's part of the joy as well as some of the frustration in our search. Why can't we just get a hold of God and really understand him, and have him in our power so that he does the things we know he ought to do? But of course, it doesn't work like that.

In his book, Capon goes on to note that when you're talking about theology—that is, seeking God—you have to be serious, but not too serious. We have to be serious because we really are looking for God—the meaning of our life, the purpose of our life, the goal that will really fulfill us. But we can't get too serious

because we're never going to catch this God. Even
the greatest theologian in the world has to finally say,
"All that I've written, all that I've ever figured out is
still not going to capture God."

The Gospels According to St. Francis is divided into
four chapters. The first is called "Francis and His Love
for the Gospel." During the course of his life, Francis
fell so in love with God and, therefore, his Word, that
he wanted nothing more than to live the Gospel. In
living the Gospel, he meant not only appreciating
the four written Gospels but all of Scripture. As we
will see, Francis uses all of Scripture to tell the Good
News about God, and especially the Good News of
God's love in the person of Jesus Christ.

The second chapter is titled "Led by the Spirit." At
the heart of Francis's spirituality was the Holy Spirit
of God, and as such, his approach to Scripture was
totally under the influence of the Spirit.

The third chapter, "The Heart of the Gospels," tells
us how Francis understood the Gospel. Here we will
try to pick up some of the basic principles Francis used
in studying Scripture. Not that he consciously formu-
lated such principles, but in explaining Scripture to
himself and his brothers he did indeed follow some
principles that we can discover and make our own.
My hope is that this will make our own approach to
Scripture that much richer.

The final chapter is called "How Francis Lived in the Gospel Light." I'll begin this chapter with one particular text that Francis uses a number of times, Matthew 12:50, focusing on his understanding of it and how it formed the foundation of his own spiritual life.

There are a few books that might be helpful to have as you read through this book. The most important of all is the Holy Scriptures. I don't recommend one version over any other, although I have used the *New Revised Standard Version* for the references in this book, except when quoting directly from the texts of St. Francis. Most of the Bible versions that you pick up today can be helpful; maybe the best way to judge them is to start reading them, and whichever one strikes home, use that.

The next book I would suggest having is *St. Francis of Assisi: Omnibus of Sources*, available through Franciscan Media. This contains the writings of St. Francis along with many of the early biographies about him. We will refer to the *Omnibus* from time to time in this book, especially to the very early biographies. Another book I highly recommend is called *Francis and Clare: The Complete Works*. It's part of a series published by Paulist Press, called the Classics of Western Spirituality.

If you find it helpful to have these books at hand, fine; if not, that's all right too.

As we go through this book and examine St. Francis of Assisi and what he tells us about Scripture, I think we will catch something like that elusive divine fox. We'll get a glimpse of what Scripture means, especially as seen through the eyes and the mind and the heart of Francis. But when we finish this book, we are not going to have it all down pat. And that's part of the beauty of this work.

What I hope we grasp from Francis is a way of looking at Scripture that will carry through the rest of our lives, always looking anew for who God is, what God is all about, and what God wants in our life. We may also come to find out how we can understand God as he makes himself known, to some extent, in both Scripture and through St. Francis.

CHAPTER ONE

Francis and His Love for the Gospel

God our Father we ask you to send your Holy Spirit into our midst and into our hearts, that this Spirit may enable us to be in union with you and with your Son. We also ask that Mary and all the angels and saints, especially Francis, will pray for us that you, Father, may enable us to realize more fully your desire that we simply be like your Son as we live our human lives, and that we might do that better if we appreciate the Word that you have given us—the Word that we read in holy Scripture. Be with us then, Father, through your Spirit and hear our prayer, which we make through Christ our Lord. Amen.

$\mathcal{A}$s we begin, let me note something very specifically about Francis's love for Scripture. It is a statistical fact that in about one hundred pages of printed text, Francis quotes or at least alludes to Scripture some six hundred times—*six hundred times in about one hundred pages of printed text*. This surely shows to us that Francis had an appreciation of Scripture, and that it always affected the way he approached his life and all of reality.

In his writings, there is a phrase that is often translated as "the written words of God," or you may find it put as, "the holy name and written words of God." This phrase simple means the words of Scripture; usually, when he uses it, he is referring to an interesting point about the Word of God.

One place where this phrase appears is in Francis's Testament, written at the end of his life as he's looking back. Here he wrote, "Wherever I come upon his most holy written words in unbecoming places, I desire to gather them up and I ask that they be collected and placed in a suitable place." Francis had such reverence for the written Word of God that if he saw a scrap of paper on the ground anywhere with the words of Scripture on them, he would treasure them and put them in a special place. In fact, in one account of the life of Francis it says, "Therefore, whenever he would find anything written, whether about God or about man, he would pick it up with the greatest reverence and put it in a sacred or discreet place."[1] Now, I'm not recommending that for our own practice—although we would be able to get rid of a lot of the litter in our world if people did that. The point is, Francis's love for Scripture was so great he did not want these words to be trampled on or ignored in any way. They needed to be treasured.

In what is called his Letter to the Entire Order, Francis repeats those same words that I just quoted from the Testament, and he indicates that, if people do this, they honor the Lord in the words that he spoke. He goes on to say, "God's words sanctify numerous objects, and it is by the power of the words of Christ that the sacrament of the altar is consecrated."[2]

Church and Scripture

Francis did not love Scripture just as some nice book that God gave us, which we know is out there and we read once in a while, but he sees it in the context of the whole Church and especially of the liturgy. It's particularly in the liturgy that the Word of God comes alive, and it becomes so alive that it gives us the gift of the Eucharist.

FRANCIS'S LOVE FOR SCRIPTURE

Perhaps one of the most beautiful descriptions of Francis's love for Scripture is given to us by St. Bonaventure. Bonaventure puts it this way,

> St. Francis had never studied Sacred Scripture, but unwearied application to prayer and the continual practice of virtue had purified his spiritual vision, so that his keen intellect was bathed in the radiance of eternal light and penetrated its depths. Free from every stain, his genius pierced to the heart of its mysteries and by affective love he entered where theologians with their science stand outside.[3]

Once he had read something in the sacred books and understood its meaning, Francis impressed it indelibly on his memory. Anything he had once grasped carefully, he meditated upon continually.

> When the friars asked him if he would allow the learned men who were entering the Order to continue the study of Sacred Scripture, he replied, "I do not mind, provided that they do not neglect prayer, after the example of Christ of whom we are told that he prayed more than he studied." It was clear that the friars should not study merely in order to have something

to say. They should study so as to practice what they have learned and then encourage others to do likewise.[4]

LIVING THE GOSPELS

The very first phrase in the Franciscan Rule reads, "The Rule and life of the Friars Minor is this, namely, to observe the Holy Gospel of our Lord Jesus Christ."[5] Discover Christ in the Gospels and all of Scripture and in a prayerful way get deeper and deeper into his mind and heart, and then you can, as Francis liked to say, "follow the footprints of our Lord Jesus Christ." That is what Francis himself wanted to do and wanted his followers to do as well. He was not satisfied simply with knowing what Scripture said or being in awe of the wonderful God that he found there, but he had to give his whole self to follow Christ and through that give his whole self to God.

Another very important text tells how Francis first decided to devote himself to living the Gospel. He was at the church of St. Mary of the Angels, his very favorite place. It was here that Francis felt he first really met God, and it became the cradle of the order. It was not only the place itself that was important, but also its connection to Mary; surely Francis's appreciation of Scripture had helped him to fall in love with Mary.

The text says that on this particular day the Gospel was Matthew 10:7–10: "As you go, proclaim the good news, 'The kingdom of heaven has come near.' Cure the sick, raise the dead, cleanse the lepers, cast out demons. You received without payment; give without payment. Take no gold, or silver, or copper in your belts, no bag for your journey, or two tunics, or sandals, or a staff; for laborers deserve their food."[6] Now these are rather important words, and we will come back to them again. But at this first hearing, Francis was so moved that after Mass, he humbly asked the priest to explain the Gospel to him more fully.

A bit of background on Francis might serve to illuminate this account. Francis knew a little bit of Latin but it was rather atrocious. Most likely, he picked up some of the words he had heard proclaimed in the Gospel, but he wasn't sure what they all meant. The priest afterward may have put these words into the Italian dialect that Francis used, and maybe gave him a little bit more of an explanation of the passage, but probably it was mostly an account of the words from Scripture.

The text then continues, "When [the priest] had set forth for Francis in order all these things, the holy Francis, hearing that the disciples of Christ should not possess gold or silver or money; nor carry along the way scrip, or wallet, or bread, or a staff; that they should not have shoes, or two tunics, but that they should preach the kingdom of God and penance, immediately cried out exultingly, 'This is what I wish, this is what I seek, this is what I long to do with all my heart.'"

Then Francis, overflowing with joy, hastened to fulfill that salutary word he had heard, and he did not suffer any delay to intervene before beginning devoutly to perform what he had heard. He immediately took off his shoes from his feet, put aside the staff from his hands, was content with one tunic, and exchanged his leather girdle for a small cord. He designed for himself a tunic that bore the likeness of the cross, that by means of it he might beat off all temptations of the devil. He designed a very rough tunic so that by it he might crucify the flesh with all its vices and sins, a very poor and mean tunic, one that would not excite the covetousness of the world.

The other things Francis had heard that day in the Gospel, however, he longed to perform with the greatest diligence and the greatest reverence. He was not a deaf hearer of the Gospel but one who committed all that he had heard to praiseworthy memory, and he tried diligently to carry it out to the letter. Even with all of the translation that has been done on the texts since Francis's time—from medieval language, from Italian to English—we still have a tremendous sense of Francis attending the Eucharist, listening to every word, and then allowing that Word of God to deepen itself right into the very bottom of his being.

In hearing that Gospel, Francis then found out how to live. He so loved the Word of God that what he heard at this moment changed his life. Really, it was changing him before this, but now he came to a new point where he discovered better what God wanted of him.

Another important point to remember here is that Francis hears this Word of God within the Eucharist and the context of the liturgy, in the context of the Church. He is not an individual hearer of the Word of God who is then going to change his own life and somehow love God and be good to the world. Francis realizes that who he is will not be understood unless he is seen as part of the Church and engaging in the actions of the Church, especially the Eucharist.

The Eucharist

In a very special way he comes alive, and the Word of God comes alive for him in the Eucharist. Francis's love for the Word of God is part of his love of the Church and of the sacraments and of the Eucharist.

Therefore, it's not too surprising that a little bit later we read of a similar incident to the one just noted, an incident that is recounted in many places. One of my favorite citations for this is found in Bonaventure's account of Francis's life, in chapter 3:3. He writes that as word spread about Francis's simple life and teachings, "certain men began to be inspired to live a life of penance."

OPENING THE GOSPELS

A man named Bernard was the first to approach Francis about following him. (Some accounts of this incident also include a man named Peter.) Francis was filled with the encouragement of the Holy Spirit when he realized he was being joined by his first follower and he said, "We shall have to ask God's advice about this." The following day they went to the Church of St. Nicholas, where they spent some time in prayer. Then Francis opened the Gospel book three times in honor of the blessed Trinity, asking God to approve Bernard's plan with the threefold testimony.

The first time the book opened to the words, "If you wish to be perfect, go, sell your possessions, and give the money to the poor" (Matthew 19:21). The second time they found the phrase, "Take nothing for your journey" (Luke 9:3). The third time they opened the Scripture, these words of our Lord caught their eyes, "If any want to become my followers, let them deny themselves and take up their cross and follow me" (Matthew 16:24). Then Francis said, "This is your life and rule. And everyone that comes to join our company must be prepared to do this. And so if you have a mind to be perfect, go home and do as you have heard."[7]

If you read this incident in some of the other biographies, there is reason to say that the way Francis did this was not by a random opening of Scripture, as Bonaventure implies. Instead, Francis went with Bernard and Peter to the priest at St. Nicholas's and said, "Find what Jesus says about how his disciples are to live a life of renouncement and dedication to the Gospel." And the priest helped them to find the passages we just read. What these accounts show is that we don't necessarily have to think that somehow God was giving special direction to Francis each time he opened the Scriptures; with God's help, Francis already knew what he was looking for.

PRAYER

Francis's love for the Scriptures made him approach the Scriptures for help. This love, which was also reverential, made him begin by first praying with his future disciples. And then in that spirit of prayer, he was able to hear the Word of God, which said, "Get rid of everything you have; don't take anything along with you; go after Christ." Simple as that. Those are the three texts guiding Francis's response to Bernard: Get rid of everything you have, don't take anything along, follow Christ. That's what it's all about.

His love and reverence for the Scripture led him to follow Christ in this way. But notice that he did this in a church and after prayer, and probably with the intervention of a priest. In this light, I'm not concerned so much about getting into the very principles of Francis's interpretation because it's so much more important to begin by seeing the atmosphere in which he came to see the Scriptures, to know the Scriptures, and to make them part of himself.

Francis is saying the most important thing to do is to be a person of prayer within the community of believers, a person who is open to God in every way God wants to come into his or her life. And if we are that way, we can go to the Scriptures and we will learn from them even if we don't apply any particular principles. I'm not saying that those cannot be helpful, but I'm saying we get nowhere simply relying on principles, especially those who follow Francis in any way. We get nowhere in anything without deepening ourselves in the Church and in prayer.

Another text that Francis quotes a number of times is John 6:63: "It is the spirit that gives life; the flesh is useless. The words that I have spoken to you are spirit and life." This quote is from Jesus talking after the miracle of the loaves and his speech on the Eucharist. Francis uses this text in several ways; one of these is in his Second Letter to All the Faithful, where he writes: "I have decided to send you a letter bringing a message with the words of our Lord Jesus Christ, who is the Word of the Father and the Holy Spirit, whose words are spirit and light."[8]

What Francis is looking for, we can describe in two ways. First of all, as Francis approaches the Scriptures, he is in touch with the Spirit of God within himself. Then, as he reads the words of God, he is going to be listening to what the Spirit says in those words. And he will be able then to listen to these words which he will call the words of Jesus Christ and the words of the Holy Spirit because, as he believed, and we believe, it is the Holy Spirit who inspires the writing of these words of Jesus. But they are words that are Spirit and life; they are words that are in touch with the Holy Spirit and give us the life of the Spirit, the life of God.

It's not just the matter of reading the Scriptures and getting beautiful thoughts, which is fine. It's also reading the Scriptures and being in touch with the Spirit in ourselves and in the words and having them change our lives. And no matter how bad we are, how far we have strayed from our true calling in Christ, they can change us. No matter how good we are, they can make us better. They need to be creative, productive in our lives. And Francis again shows his love for Scripture when he says that the words there are Spirit and life.

Let me just note a few words of reflection on all of this. Francis did have a great reverence for Scripture, but it was not an idolatrous reverence. He was not so absolutely tied to the words of Scripture as to make the words more important than the God to whom they were leading.

Now I bring that up because that is a danger sometimes. First, we want to get people to really love the Scriptures and reverence them and use them. And then all of a sudden you find people using the words of Scripture as if every sentence is an absolute statement from God about everything and thinking that they're going to find all the answers of life directly in those words. No Scripture will do that.

The words of Scripture are like the sacraments, especially the sacrament of baptism. We use the water, and the water cleanses us, not because it's water but because God is using that symbol along with the words of Scripture to bring himself to us. We don't worship the water; we worship God. We don't worship the words of Scripture; we worship God. We cannot look at Scripture and come to petrify it. It is not like the Petrified Forest—as if we've got everything solidified now, and nothing else can be said about it.

Scripture does not have automatic answers to everything. Even where it has some profound doctrinal points, it still is not saying everything about God. Through the Scriptures, we glimpse the divine fox here and there, as I mentioned in the introduction to this book, but we don't capture him. We can't capture God in the Scriptures, but we can come in touch with God.

And that's the beauty of the Word of God. If we could come to the point where we say, "I have it all understood, and I have it all in this little ball, and that's the end of it," what good would it be? We would have to find some other ball to play with because our human nature needs something that will grow—make us grow more and more all the time—and that is the way Scripture can work. It's hinting at God, giving us glimpses of God, helping us to learn better how to live, a little bit more of what God wants of us. But it doesn't give us all the answers nicely manufactured, all set out. We worship God, not the written words. But we reverence the words of God because they lead us to God himself. We pray.

And so maybe the way I would like to end this chapter is by suggesting that, as we approach Scripture in the spirit of Francis, we might try to make his words our own. When we hear those words, we might say, "This is what I wish, this is what I seek, this is what I long to do with all my heart."

CHAPTER TWO

Led by the Spirit

O great and glorious God and my Lord Jesus Christ, send your Spirit into our midst that he may enlighten our minds and inflame our hearts, that he may give us a right faith, a certain hope, and a perfect charity. In this way, through this Spirit, we pray that we may be able to understand the Word of God given to us in the Scriptures by the Holy Spirit, and that as he dwells in our hearts, he may bring us closer to you and closer to all our brothers and sisters in the world today. We ask that you hear this prayer and grant it through Christ our Lord. Amen.[9]

In the previous chapter, I pointed out not only Francis's love for Scripture, but also that he understood it and approached it and appreciated and lived it in the context of the Church. You might say that his love for Scripture was really part of his love for the Church. Not only that, but as he approached the Scriptures, he did so in the context of prayer. Recall how he first prayed and then opened the Scriptures to discover how God wanted him to follow Christ.

On another occasion he heard the Gospel during the celebration of the Eucharist and was moved by it, and so we see that the Word of God, in Francis's mind, was closely associated with the Eucharist—indeed, with all of the sacraments. Francis did not just come as an individual to find out how he and God should relate, but rather how he, as a human being with all these relationships, might be able to come to God. And it is in that context that he experienced his great love for Scripture.

In John 6:63 Jesus, after speaking about the Eucharist, says that his words are "spirit and life." Francis insists that in the Scriptures the Spirit is speaking and that Spirit is coming in order to bring life to Francis—actually, to anyone who would read the Scriptures with faith.

SERVICE TO ALL

In paragraph 193 of Thomas Celano's biography of Francis, we read, "Francis wished that the Order should be for the poor and unlearned, not only for the rich and wise." Francis himself said, "With God there [is] no respect for persons." In other words, the Holy Spirit rests equally upon the poor and the simple. Francis even wanted this thought inserted into his Rule, but since it already had been approved by a papal bull, this could not be done. Nevertheless, it is significant that Francis wanted the Holy Spirit to be thought of and experienced as the real minister general of the order.

To better appreciate, let's look at what a minister general is in case you are not acquainted with that title. "Minister general" is the title Francis gives to the supreme authority of his Order. Other orders might call this person a supreme moderator or maybe a supreme abbot or even a master general. But Francis insisted that the one who had the highest authority was a minister, a servant of all the rest.

This rationale is deeply in touch with the whole tradition of Scripture; we might also say with all of Scripture and all of tradition. Jesus tells his disciples that they are not to lord it over one another as those who are kings and emperors do, but rather they are to serve one another. They are to minister to one another and even wash one another's feet. And this was no mere theoretical rumination on Jesus's part: His life gave us the ultimate example of this. Jesus is the supreme servant of the Church, of the world, and of all of history. Francis too made this model his own, and it is really the tradition of the Church that anyone who is in authority is the servant of the rest. This does not deny that all members of the Church must be obedient; even Francis insists on obeying the minister general, obeying the pope, and so on.

But the whole spirit of authority needs to be grounded in service, and the best tradition of the Church is that way too. Pope Gregory the Great first used that phrase most of the popes since then have used when they begin a letter: "The servant of the servants of God...." That's what the supreme authority is.

Some years ago there was a column in the *National Catholic Reporter* that contained several sentences that express this well: "The Pope is the servant of the servants of God. Bishops are servants of the servant of the servants of God, and priests are servants of the servants of the servant of the servants of God. And lay people have servant problems." Maybe this is a little cynical, maybe a little sarcastic, but it touches on the real rich tradition of the Church: The servant of God is the servant of all.

Francis understood that best through the Scriptures and through what the Church had to offer at that time. And surely, as we look at the history of the Church, we do see some of its leaders who embrace the role of servant. There's one pope who made it to the chair of Peter by political machinations and said, "Now we have got the papacy, let us enjoy it." Fortunately, that's not the predominate feeling of most about authority in the Church. But it does point out that there are individuals down through history who have not quite been able to see themselves as real servants of the Church.

So this is what Francis means when he says, "The Holy Spirit is the real minister general of the order." It gives us an insight into how the Holy Spirit not only affects the Franciscan order as a whole but all the individuals in the order—as well as in the Church.

THE SPIRIT AND PRAYER

As we look at the way Francis loved and was loved by the Spirit, we come to see that, as he understood the Scriptures, the Holy Spirit does not come in and force things; rather, the Holy Spirit himself serves each of us. In another place, when he's praying to God, Francis says, "You are humility."[10] We don't often hear "humility" expressed as an attribute of God, but it is indeed an attribute of God. And Francis helps us to see that it's a particular attribute of the Holy Spirit as well. The Holy Spirit is humility. The Holy Spirit is our servant as we try to understand the Scriptures. That is what Francis is driving at a number of times in his writing.

Many Franciscans today live by a later version of Francis's Rule, abbreviated as the Rule of 1223. This is the Rule approved by the Church by which all Franciscans of the First Order are to live—Friars Minor, Friars Minor Conventual, and Friars Minor Capuchin. It is in this later Rule that Francis is saying how he is in tune with the Holy Spirit, what the Holy Spirit is supposed to mean to our lives.

In Chapter 10 of the Rule of 1223, we read this: "They [friars] should realize instead that the only thing they should desire is to have the Spirit of God at work within them while they pray to him unceasingly with a heart free from self-interest."[11] This is Francis telling us all, "Be open to the Holy Spirit." That's the most important thing in the life of a friar. Be open to the Holy Spirit; try to have him be an intimate part of your life.

We can't force the Spirit in, but he wants to come in. It's up to us simply to do what we can to be open to that Spirit. We want to have the Holy Spirit and his holy manner of working living within us, energizing us. It's the very principle of our living. That holy manner of working which the Spirit carries on within us—that's the whole purpose of our lives: to be open to the Spirit and allow him to have his effect upon us.

There is a similar passage in this same Rule, Chapter 5, and here Francis tells his First Order that they are to avoid idleness, the enemy of the soul, so that they do not extinguish the spirit of holy prayer and devotion to which all other things of our earthly existence must contribute. So do not extinguish the Spirit; Paul tells that to the Thessalonians, too: "Do not quench the Spirit" (5:19). Don't extinguish him; allow him to live in you. Not only that, but everything else should go in the direction of allowing that Spirit to bring about prayer and devotion in our lives. This means saying words from our innermost self, with sentiments of love and adoration and praise and petition, and also with deep devotion. Devotion means the self-giving of all our lives, giving everything we are and have to our God.

What Francis's Rule is saying about the Holy Spirit is that, when we come to Scripture and apply it to our lives, Scripture itself will be a real source of devotion, of prayer, of real living for God if we have the Holy

Spirit within us. We discover the Spirit speaking to us in the words of Scripture, and it is the Spirit within us who enables us to listen to him. It's a rather interesting concept but quite true. The Spirit is present in the Word; the Spirit is present in us.

If we are like Francis, prayerful, appreciative of belonging to the body of Christ, the Church, the community of believers, and really surrendering ourselves to the Spirit present in Scripture, then the Holy Spirit present within us will enable us to be much more open to understanding the Word and to having it be really effective in bringing about a holy working in our lives.

Another place where we can get a better grasp of this is in the First Admonition of St. Francis. He had twenty-eight Admonitions in all, and some people have described them as being Francis's equivalent to the Sermon on the Mount. The very first of the Admonitions, not surprisingly, is about the Body of Christ, about the Eucharist.

In this Admonition Francis begins with a number of quotations from Sacred Scripture, starting with John 14:6–9:

> Our Lord Jesus told his disciples, "I am the way, and the truth, and the life. No one comes to the Father but through me. If you

had known me, you would also have known my Father. And henceforth you do know him, and you have seen him." Philip said to him, "Lord, show us the Father, and it is enough for us." Jesus said to him, "Have I been so long a time with you, and you have not known me? Philip, he who sees me sees also the Father."[12]

Then Francis refers to 1 Timothy 6:16, where we hear that the Father dwells in light inaccessible. This is followed by a quotation from John 4:24, "God is spirit," then back to John 1:18, "No one at any time has seen God." Now that may seem mixed up, but if you put those three quotes together you will begin to see what Francis is talking about. The Father lives in inaccessible light, and God is spirit, and no one has ever seen God.

So God is spiritual. We cannot see him; we cannot see the Father in his own self, in his spiritual nature. But Francis continues: "It is the spirit that gives life; the flesh profits nothing. The words that I have spoken to you are spirit and life" (John 6:63). But then Francis adds, "But God the Son is equal to the Father and so he too can be seen only in the same way as the Father and the Holy Spirit." Do you see what he's getting at? We don't see the Father except in the Spirit, and we don't see God the Son in his divinity.

We see Jesus. But we do not see his divine character except in the Spirit. And so, in a sense, God the Son is just as invisible as the Father and the Spirit.

Francis then takes these statements and their implications, and goes on to apply them to two situations. First of all, everybody in Palestine could see the human Jesus, but only some came to believe that he was the Son of God. Why? It was the Spirit alone who enabled them to be believers. The only way they could discover that this human Jesus was really God is because the Spirit enabled them to see beyond the flesh to the divine person behind it. Francis then applies these Scripture passages in another way, noting that in the Eucharist we see bread and wine, but only some believe that it is the Body and Blood of Jesus. Again, it's only the Spirit who enables them so to believe.

We can apply this same pattern to Scripture. Francis was led, we might say, by the Spirit not only to recognize God the Father and God the Son and the presence of the Spirit, but also that through the Spirit he was able to go to the Scriptures and understand them for what they were really saying. Everybody can read the words in the Bible, but only some discover there the Word of God and the meaning of that Word. And again, only the Spirit enables us to discover that in the Scriptures, God is speaking to us, and to discover what it is that God is saying to us in Scripture.

In his Letter to All the Faithful, Francis writes, "I have decided to send you a letter bringing a message with the words of our Lord Jesus Christ, who is the Word of the Father, and of the Holy Spirit, whose words are spirit and life."[13] The implication is that it will take the guidance of the Spirit in our minds and hearts to discover in the scriptural Word what the Holy Spirit wants to say to us, and then receive the life he wants to give us. The words of Scripture are Spirit and life; the Spirit is there to give us life. We will be able to receive the life of the Spirit when we allow the Spirit to lead us.

In his earlier Rule in Chapter 22, Francis again quotes John 6:64: "Jesus' words are spirit and life" and then John 14:6 "Jesus is the way, and the truth, and the life," and then he goes on, "And so we must hold fast to the words, the life, and the teaching and the holy Gospel of our Lord Jesus Christ."[14] It begins with the Spirit and goes through all of the experiences of Francis, his whole approach to Scripture and to Christ, to the Gospel, and ends leading Francis to live the Gospel. Having been led by the Spirit, Francis understands the Gospel and then eventually is able to live the Gospel. From all of this we can begin to grasp something of Francis's scriptural spirituality and something of his approach to the Scriptures.

I'm still not trying to break down Francis's approach into different rules of interpretation—we'll do that in another chapter. Here, I want to emphasize that we'll never understand Scripture unless we come out of prayer, come out of the Spirit, come out of our living, into the Word of God, which will give us the insight that we need. Then other rules can be helpful. If we come with the guidance of the Spirit and spirit of humility, depending on the Spirit to lead us and even serve us, we will be able to discover what God tells us in the Scriptures.

Maybe we can put it together this way. The Scriptures are the Word of God. Indeed, they are in a special way the Word of the Holy Spirit; God speaks to us in no superficial way. As he read the Scriptures, Francis realized he was being addressed by the Spirit of God, and he realized that he will hear what the Spirit tells him in the Scriptures only if he listens to the Spirit in his own mind and heart. Thus Francis cultivates a life of prayer and listens to the Scriptures in the context of worship and as a member of the body of Christ.

Francis realizes that his grasp of the sacred Scriptures is not to end with a mere abstract understanding.

The words are Spirit and life. He hears the Spirit and then lives out what the Spirit says. That is what he is driving at when he tells his brothers, "And so we must hold fast to the words, the life, the teaching, and the holy Gospel of our Lord Jesus Christ."[15]

In this context, we might look here at Admonition Seven, which is called by some Francis's basic rule for interpretation. This Admonition reads,

> St. Paul tells us "The letter kills, but the spirit gives life" (2 Cor 3:6). A man has been killed by the letter when he wants to know quotations only so that people will think he is very learned and he can make money to give to their relatives and friends. A religious has been killed by the letter when he has no desire to follow the spirit of Sacred Scripture, but wants to know what it says only so that he can explain it to others. On the other hand, those have received life from the spirit of Sacred Scripture who, by their words and example, refer to the most high God, to whom belongs all good.[16]

That last sentence may sound a bit fuzzy. What Francis seems to be saying here is, when we approach a text, it is not in order to grasp it in such a way that people will think we're smart because we can interpret it very nicely and bring some kind of praise upon ourselves. No, what we need to do in reading Scripture and understanding it is to really appreciate it and to give thanks to the Most High God to whom every good belongs. That, I think, is telling us something of the way Francis approached Scripture. But it still may seem to be just a general presentation, and I think we need to try to go beyond that. To that end I have picked out five Admonitions of St. Francis.

FRANCIS'S ADMONITIONS

Let's look at these Admonitions and see how Francis used Scripture. Just a brief sidenote here: Francis is giving these Admonitions to his own brothers, and so he uses *he*, *him*, and other male references, but it could just as well refer to *she* and *her*. Please understand it that way.

In the Eighth Admonition, there are two quotations from Scripture. The apostle says, "No one can say Jesus is Lord except in the Holy Spirit (1 Cor 12:3), and there is no one who does good, not even one (Rom 3:12)." Now what does Francis get out of this? Here's his conclusion: "And so when a man envies his brother the good God says or does through him, it is like committing a sin of blasphemy, because he is really envying God, who is the only source of every good."[17]

Francis comments on the text from Romans, "There is no one who does good." What he sees St. Paul driving at is that we cannot do good on our own. Whatever good I do, whatever good you do, whatever good anybody does is not our own doing; it is only the doing of God. In fact, the other quotation cited in the preceding paragraph brings that out in one particular way: "No one can say Jesus is Lord except in the Holy Spirit." So we cannot even say, "Jesus is Lord," and really mean it from the depths of our being that Jesus is the glorified Lord to whom we owe our whole lives and to whom we want to belong—except that the Holy Spirit enables us to do so.

This is an example of Francis putting two seemingly disparate Scripture texts together in a very interesting way. Certainly, Francis saw that it was easy for his own brothers to be envious of the good that others would do, but he's helping us to see this from a scriptural perspective. He's helping his brothers to see that any good that happens is the gift of God, and therefore, there is no reason to be envious of another. To envy would mean we wish that good did not exist; yet the good that exists is God's doing. We are wishing that God was not good, and that is why this envy is blasphemy. If envy is a problem for you, this might be some helpful advice.

The Ninth Admonition concerns true love. Again, notice the quotation Francis uses, "Our Lord says in the Gospel, 'Love your enemies,'" taken from the Scripture quote, "Love your enemies and pray for those who persecute you" (Matthew 5:44). This is part of the Sermon on the Mount, which starts at the beginning of Matthew 5 with the Beatitudes.

Now what does Francis understand by these words? Again, let's think of him as being led by the Spirit, trying really to be prayerful and discovering what God is telling him. He might have intended it as the inspiration for a person who truly loves his enemy, who is not upset at any injury that is done to himself, but out of love of God is disturbed at the sin of the others. Perhaps Francis saw that his brothers were having a lot of arguments and fights among themselves. (The Order hasn't changed a whole lot; that still happens today once in a while!)

Francis is trying to help his brothers to deal with their conflicts by saying that the brothers should, out of love of God, not get upset because your brother hurt you personally, but do get concerned and be disturbed because he's hurting himself by hating you; that's what Francis is telling his brothers to do. Appreciate that your brother, that poor man, is hurting himself, leading to a worse kind of existence;

he will be in misery and eventually cut himself off from his brothers in this life and in the next. That's what we should be concerned about. So when we love our enemies, Francis says, we love them even though they hurt us. We are concerned because they are sinning, and that is what we want to help them overcome.

The Thirteenth Admonition deals with patience. It is based on a quotation from the Sermon on the Mount, one of the Beatitudes: "Blessed are the peacemakers, for they will be called children of God" (Matthew 5:9). Francis comments that a person cannot know how much patience and humility he has within himself as long as everything goes well with him. But when the time comes when those who should do him justice do quite the opposite to him, he has only as much patience and humility as he has on that occasion and no more.

It's easy to go to a deserted island and not get impatient with anybody, but we don't live on deserted islands. And any real Christian is caught up in all kinds of relationships; Francis is aware of this. Here he is particularly talking to his own brothers and their own relationships when he tells us, in effect, "If you're living with all really nice people who always do everything you want, well, you're not proving too much.

But it's when things don't go right, that's when you discover how really patient you are and how much of a peacemaker you really want to be."

Admonition Sixteen refers to purity of heart: "Blessed are the clean of heart, for they shall see God" (Matthew 5:8). Francis notes that the truly clean of heart are those who have no time for the things of this world and seek the things of heaven. These people never cease to adore and behold the Lord God, living and true with a pure heart and soul. Here I think I need to do a little explanation of Francis. In those days—and this is relevant in our days too—some ascetics speak of despising the things of earth. This does not mean that Francis or any real Christian ever saw the things of earth as evil; these are things God created. The point is that the things of earth are to serve and help toward the worship of God and the love of God and doing of the will of God. In that sense, when we say we despise the things of earth, we despise the times they take us away from God.

It's helpful to note here that Francis is close to what most modern interpreters would say about this text, too. In fact, his Scripture interpretations in the other Admonitions are close enough as well.

What do we mean by "clean of heart" here? A lot of people think of that in terms of chastity, and indeed chastity is one of the things that makes us pure of heart. But to be pure of heart in the biblical sense means, above all, to have our eyes focused straight on God, or as some of the Scripture texts translate that today, to be single-minded. In other words, blessed are the single-minded, the people who take whatever happens in their lives and focus it all toward God. They are single-mindedly concerned about worshipping God in every possible way they can.

Admonition Twenty-Eight is entitled "Virtue should be concealed or it will be lost." "Blessed the religious who treasures up for heaven (cf. Mt 6:20) the favors God has given him and does not want to show off for what he can get out of them." This is really more an allusion to Scripture that an actual quotation. In Matthew 6:20, Jesus tells his disciples not to seek treasures that the moth and rust consume, but seek the treasure of heaven. Francis is interpreting this text in his own way, saying that a person is blessed if he keeps the wonderful things God has done in his life as a hidden treasure. You don't go blabbing it all over the place, "See what God does for me, see what God does for me?"

Francis is concerned that we might use those kinds of experiences—the wonderful things that God has done for us—to lead us to pride in our lives, to putting ourselves up as better than others. The Admonition goes on, then, that we should not reveal these things to others in the hope of profiting, for God himself will manifest his deeds to whomever he wishes. Again, it's getting back to the point made earlier: Whatever good we accomplish is God's doing in us.

And we don't have to trumpet it about. As Jesus said, "So whenever you give alms, do not sound a trumpet before you, as the hypocrites do in the synagogues and in the streets, so that they may be praised by others" (Matthew 6:2). It's something of that idea that Francis is picking up. And he continues, "Blessed the religious who keeps God's marvelous doings in his heart." Here he alludes to Luke 2:51: "His mother treasured all these things in her heart." It's fitting to end this Admonition with that particular reference, because it is a reference to Mary, and I have not said much about Mary yet.

If there is anyone who is dear to Francis, it is Mary; she's the one who treasured these things and pondered them in her heart, and that is exactly what Francis is saying here. We don't go about spouting to everybody all the wonderful things that we have done or that God has done in us. We treasure them in our heart. Of course, there's nothing wrong, as we do experience this goodness of God, if we then begin to share it more fully with others. But we don't make a big point about saying, "See what God did here, see what God did there?"

THE BIBLE AND OUR LIVES

Now that we've taken a look at how Francis approached Scripture with the Holy Spirit in his mind and heart, trying to see what the Spirit says, let's get away from what Francis said about these texts and see what they might mean to us. What Francis says can be helpful to us, but we want to make the Scriptures personal in a very real way. To do this, we approach as Francis would, in a spirit of prayer, depending on the Holy Spirit to see more of what these texts might mean to us. It's relatively easy to begin to apply Scripture to everyday life, especially if we come to grips with some of the concrete details of our own lives.

But first, let's go back to the First Admonition. Of the two quotations that Francis refers to, I'll begin with the second one because I think it is the foundation to the other. "There is no one who does good, not even one." In our own experience, most of us would have some trouble accepting those words. In fact, we have done some good things in our lives, and maybe we even feel that we have done them ourselves. We certainly have put effort into doing some of the good things that we do. But our faith leads us beyond this.

The Holy Spirit helps us to go beyond our own immediate impressions when we sense that as human beings we are helpless. How can I take my next breath except that God is sustaining me? He did not just create us some years ago, or he didn't just make us part of the creation that came to be billions of years ago. God is always creating, always keeping in existence. And so our very ability to live is a constant gift. All the more then, to be aware that if there is anything good that we do, it's not anything that we ourselves do but rather what God does in us.

We also recognize that we do some wrong things, and we know that we can overcome the wrong and do good only because we have God's help. That's where I see the other quotation coming in: "No one can say Jesus is Lord except in the Holy Spirit."

To say that Jesus is Lord means that this person we know as Jesus suffered and died on the cross and then rose again and is in glory with God. But how is that real to us? How can we really believe that? Again it seems like we can say the words easily enough. But can we really mean them and live them out except by having the gift of the Holy Spirit? With the Spirit's help, we can dedicate ourselves to the will of God as Jesus did.

When I believe that of myself, I can believe that of others and be led by Francis to see that everyone's life, every good that anybody does is the gift of God's Spirit. Therefore, all the good I see around me is God acting. And not only should I follow Francis and not envy that good, but I can go beyond all of that and see that everyone's good is a manifestation of the action of the Holy Spirit. The holy working of the Holy Spirit that Francis talks about being in each one of us is then permeating all human beings in some way. So should I not be led to appreciate that, not only the good that is done in myself, but the good all around me is God's gift to me?

What about the Ninth Admonition, and the quotation there: "Love your enemies (Mt 5:44)." That always reminds me of a priest friend of mine, who used to say, "I don't think we should preach that to our people. Let's just get people to love their friends; that's hard enough."

That saying reminds me that we should start where we have our first problem; maybe it's even loving ourselves. If we really could come in touch with ourselves—not independent of God but because of the good that God is doing in us—and see that God even overcomes the evil that's in us, maybe we can begin to love ourselves. Maybe we can even believe that evil does tend to hang around us all, that the darkness within us will, we presume, be with us all the time, that even with this knowledge we still can love ourselves.

Sometimes when we truly face the darkness in ourselves and become aware of the things we have done wrong, feelings may rise up that could tend to scare us or lead us in the wrong direction. If we can face them squarely and say, "God is with me; God knows that these things are there," then we begin to know we are not alone in dealing with the darkness in our lives. Perhaps we can even embrace this darkness as part of what makes us grow as human beings.

As we really face our selfishness, as we really face our unjust angers, as we really face the grudges that we hold, as we really face the bitterness that is there, we don't have to sweep it under the carpet. We can look at it and know that God loves us as we are and is willing to help us grow beyond these faults and failings. If we really believe that God loves us exactly as we are now, we can love ourselves. And if we can love ourselves with all that we see within us, shouldn't we also be able to love our friends, our neighbors, the people we live with, our families, even those who have grudges against us, because we can see them as people like ourselves: struggling, making mistakes, but still loved by God?

And then, if we can do that, love those people who are not really enemies, we can even be led to love those who really hate us, who persecute us, who blame us. In our world today, there are a lot of people like that; maybe some of them even hate us because they have good reason to. Many of us have a way of life that a lot of people can't—people who hardly have enough to eat, who don't have the material things that we do, who don't have the freedom we have in our lives. They have reason to hate us. Maybe instead of getting all upset when some people in those circumstances rebel and get mean, we might try to understand that they're simply rebelling from a situation that is oppressing and demeaning and dehumanizing them.

As we look at the world today, for example, we see people who own companies in other countries. The owners are wealthy, yet they give the workers less than a living wage, sometimes making their employees work in oppressive conditions, simply to be profitable at the expense of the workers. Here we can't only love the people being oppressed, but we must love even their oppressors. These are the people Jesus tells us to love. Can I love them into a new vision of the world in which they see the most important thing is not profit, but human beings?

The Thirteenth Admonition is entitled "Patience."

"Blessed are the peacemakers for they will be called children of God (Mt 5:9). Francis sees this as almost a one-on-one situation, one individual with another. God knows we do need peace in this world, however. How are we going to achieve it? Maybe as we read this text, we come to realize we need to know a lot more about peace and justice and how to judge what's going on in our world. How do we come to really understand the news that comes to us each day, the words of the politicians and authorities, and the way they deal with things? I can't really be a peacemaker unless I make a lot more effort to understand what's going on in our world today.

But I also have to understand that, if I listen to the Holy Spirit, I have a much better chance of really becoming a peace-loving person myself and finding ways of bringing peace to our world today. And if there's anything that will give me comfort, maybe it will be doing this because I'm assured that I will be a child of God: Blessed are the peacemakers, for they will be called the children of God." It's worth the effort. It's what God our Father really wants. It's something that I can really want, but I need to do an awful lot of soul searching, really listening to the Spirit and try to come up with new ways of bringing peace.

We don't need just to look at the general situation of the world for this either. So many of us need peace in our own hearts, in our neighborhoods. If we find ways of becoming peaceful ourselves, we will discover how better to bring peace to the world.

Peace: After all, what does it mean? It means to be whole, together. Ultimately, in our Christian understanding, to be at peace means to be one with God. If I do become a person of prayer who loves myself and then is willing to love others that same way, I will find ways to bring peace. This sounds nice, but we also know that we can get into situations where we have misunderstandings and bitterness and gossip, people talking about us and against us. Sometimes it feels like the best thing to do is to retaliate.

We hear so much of that happening; it seems that's what the world runs on. When we are hurt, we want to get even. That's not being a peacemaker. But if I want to be a child of God, I have to remember that God sends his rain and his sunshine on the just and the unjust alike (see Matthew 5:45). He does good to all indiscriminately. So no matter how somebody has hurt me, the Holy Spirit can enable me to bring peace, the love of God, and his goodness to others.

Purity of heart, singleness of mind, means focusing my vision totally on God. Looking only to God is the purpose, the goal, and the meaning of my life. If I have that kind of vision, if I really look that way I'll see God as Jesus tells me: "Blessed are the pure in heart for they will see God" (Matthew 5:8). There again, look at all the things in our lives that tend to draw us in different directions: "I have to go to this place and see this new thing, I have to acquire these new clothes, I have to make an impression over here." We get so caught up in pleasing ourselves and pleasing other people that we forget God.

Here again Francis gives us good guidance when he says simply, "My God and my all." That's being pure of heart; that's being single-minded. I look totally to God, and when I discover God and find that he is everything, I can embrace everything else. To be single-minded and have my vision totally fixed on God is not to forget his world, but to embrace it with his love. We discover that to be pure of heart does not make us lonely and alone, but makes us one with everything God has made—ultimately, one with God himself. That is being at peace: being one with God and embracing his whole world.

In the Sermon on the Mount, when Jesus tells us to store up treasure in heaven, we might think, "Well, I'm going to get a lot of merits here and build them up, and God's going to have a treasure chest up in heaven, and I'll keep adding to that." Is that what God really means? *Heaven* is often simply used instead of the name of God, so what Jesus is really talking about is that we are to put all our treasure in God. God is our treasure, and no moth can consume that, no rust can corrode that, because God cannot be hurt by any corrupting influences.

If our whole treasure is in God, we will be in him and we will partake in the very life of God himself. We will possess some of God's goodness. It's not so much that we're going to pile up wonderful things and place them with God, but simply that God is going to take us to himself and make us his treasure. That's the great dignity we have as human beings made by God and as Christians who follow Christ.

Mary, Model for Francis and for Ourselves

Maybe the best way to do this is by making Mary our model, as Francis does when he says, "Blessed is the servant who keeps the secrets of the Lord in his heart." Mary kept all these things in her heart, treasured them, meditated on them, allowed them to come to life in herself. What Mary especially treasured in her heart was related to the experiences connected with the birth of Jesus and his early life. She kept trying to discover more and more what those experiences really meant. And that's the kind of treasure we can have.

The Holy Spirit is within us, calling us to think about God, see where God really is and what God is saying in his Word. Gradually, the realization builds within us that God is our Father, Jesus is our brother, and the Spirit gives us a share in the divine life. We can experience always the great mysteries of God's love and his salvation in Christ. Mary spent her life treasuring these things, and we can also.

CHAPTER THREE

The Heart of the Gospels

O great and glorious God and my Lord Jesus Christ, send your Spirit into our midst that he may enlighten our minds and inflame our hearts, that he may give us a right faith, a certain hope, and a perfect charity. In this way, through this Spirit, we pray that we may be able to understand the Word of God given to us in the Scriptures by the Holy Spirit, and that as he dwells in our hearts, he may bring us closer to you and closer to all our brothers and sisters in the world today. We ask that you hear this prayer and grant it through Christ our Lord. Amen.

*U*p to now we have looked at Francis's love for Scripture and how his love for Scripture was in the context of his life in the Church. We have seen that this love came out of his own personal prayer life, which not only helped him to love the Scriptures but also to understand them better.

Francis realized that the Holy Spirit was critically important in his life. He would have made the Holy Spirit the minister general of his order; that's the way he wanted his followers to see it. And since the minister general is the universal servant, the Holy Spirit then is, then, the servant of all. He is the servant by giving us God's Word, and he is the servant within us who enables us to understand God's Word. Francis wanted his followers to know that everything he did would lead to and contribute to the spirit of prayer and devotion, to which everything was to be subordinated.

Now let's take the next step and see how Francis understood the Gospel. We have already done that to some extent, but now we will come down to some more basic principles, some things that we might spell out a little bit more clearly. Some of these principles, you might say, are human principles, and yet all of these are under the guidance of the Spirit.

To begin, I would like to refer to a modern martyr, Franz Jägerstätter, who was born in 1907 and died in 1943. He was an Austrian farmer, and when the Nazis came in to take over Austria as an annex to Germany, they held a plebiscite, which is a direct vote of all the members of an electorate on an important public question. They asked the people, "Do you want this?" Of course, the people really had no choice in the matter and so all the people voted for it. Except Jägerstätter; he did not vote for it.

Jägerstätter knew that the next thing the Nazis would want to do is bring him into their army, and that too he refused to do. Now here is a man who is thirty-six years old, with a wife and three daughters; he knew that, if he refused to go into the German army, he would be killed. But he could not see any reason or any excuse to do anything else except refuse.

What makes this story all the more poignant is that his pastor said to him, "You're a husband, you're a father, you owe things to your family. To go into the German army and thereby save your life and be able to take care of your family will be perfectly all right." But he could not believe his pastor. The bishop of the diocese even talked to him, and said it would be all right: "It is not a sin for you to join the German army." But again, he did not listen to the bishop.

Jägerstätter was thrown in prison, where the prison chaplains tried to tell him the same thing as his priest and bishop: Join the German army to save your family. Again he refused. Finally, in August of 1943 he was put to death. While he was in prison, shortly before his death, he had received a picture from his family with his three daughters holding a banner, and on that banner it said, "Dear Father, come home soon." But Jägerstätter refused to change his approach. He would not join the German army. He was a man who was completely convinced that what the Nazis were doing was totally against the Gospel, and therefore, totally against everything he believed in.

Franz Jägerstätter died totally opposed to all that Nazism stood for. This was at a time when the Austrian Church had let herself be taken prisoner by giving uncritical support to Nazi rule. This support extended to the very end of the war. Every priest from whom Franz ever sought counsel considered his actions to be an unwise and unnecessary sacrifice. All of them advised him that, as far as his personal obligations were concerned, the order of priority began with his duties as a husband, a father, a loyal citizen. Moreover, they told him he had neither the competence nor the right to challenge the government concerning the morality or immorality of the war in which he was asked to serve.

That is a very brief account of one man's struggle with Nazism, which resulted in his death. Pope Benedict XVI declared Jägerstätter a martyr and, October 26, 2007, Jägerstätter was beatified. His feast day is the day of his christening, May 21. I use this story as an attempt to say something in a modern setting about what Francis himself did when he approached the Gospels. He looked at the Gospels and took them seriously, and he made up his mind that, no matter what anybody thought, he was going to live this Gospel. He was going to listen to the Spirit in the words and in himself, and no matter what the consequences, he was going to be faithful to the Gospel.

Jagerstatter joined the secular Franciscans toward the end of his life. I think his conduct shows what Francis might easily have done if he were in Jägerstätter's place in 1943 in Austria.

That leads me to look at Francis's own life again to find an example of how he dealt with the Gospel. I'll refer once again to the account in Thomas Celano's biography of Francis, which tells of how he heard Matthew 10:7–10 read at Mass. It's worthwhile to recall that at this point in time, Francis had very recently rebuilt the church of St. Mary of the Angels.

It was fast becoming his favorite church, obviously because of the connection to the Mother of God.

As Francis listens to the Gospel, he hears these words: "As you go, proclaim the good news, 'The kingdom of heaven has come near.' Cure the sick, raise the dead, cleanse the lepers, cast out demons. You received without payment; give without payment. Take no gold, or silver, or copper in your belts, no bag for your journey, or two tunics, or sandals, or a staff; for laborers deserve their food." The workman, after all, is worth his keep. Recall that, when Francis heard these words, he asked the priest for further explanation, and the priest probably translated the words into the language that Francis knew better, namely, the Italian of his day, which undoubtedly gave some further understanding to Francis.

When Francis heard what this text really meant, he said, "This is what I wish, this is what I seek, this is what I long to do with all my heart." Then Francis changed his garb and went forth, announcing the kingdom of God. He wanted to do everything that he heard in the Gospel, going about preaching penance, always beginning with a greeting of peace. All this had occurred within the context of prayer and the context of worship, the celebration of the Eucharist.

Francis hears the Word announced at that time and in the church, a church that is dedicated to Mary and which also represents for Francis the whole Church community. He's listening to the Word in his community and, as he hears those words, he hears them very much as spoken to himself. Here God his Father is telling him something. Here Francis hears Jesus, who told the apostles how to go forth and preach the Gospel, talking to Francis himself. He hears the Spirit of God who is behind these words and also comes into contact with the Spirit in his own self. The words are Spirit and life; it's the Holy Spirit who is there bringing life to Francis through the words that he spoke.

As Francis hears the Father, the Son, and the Spirit speaking to him, he accepts the call. He hears the call in those words and discovers, "This is what God wants of me" and he decides to go ahead and do it. He went and began to preach penance.

Principles of Interpretation

You might say this is an overall picture of what happened. But by looking at it a little more closely, we can come up with an understanding of what Francis did when he heard those words. I have them lined up in five words to describe his principles of interpretation: *literal, realistic, personal, practical,* and *spiritual.* If we understand what those five words suggest we get an insight into Francis's own way of understanding Scripture. I would suggest you keep those five words in mind any time you read Scripture, as well—especially as we look at what these five words meant to Francis.

The first word is *literal*; I use that word in opposition to *allegorical*. Allegory is telling a story in which every element in the story is supposed to tell you a spiritual truth. That's not a bad way of approaching Scripture at times. In fact, if it's done in a restrained way, it can help us gain insight into Scripture. Some of the early Church Fathers used an allegorical method to interpret Scripture; in fact, this practice continued down into the Middle Ages. But by Francis's time, allegory was sometimes taken to the extreme. By looking at Scripture in a literal way, we can appreciate what Francis is doing by comparing that to what some of these allegorists have done.

In a book that was contemporary to Francis's time, for instance, when the author looks at the Scripture passage about not taking gold or silver or any money along for the journey, he says, "No, there is a true gold and a false gold. The true gold is the wisdom of God; the false gold is earthly wisdom." Then he concludes that, as Jesus is sending his disciples out, he tells them, "Don't take the false gold." Surely they can take the true gold of the wisdom of God, but they must avoid the false gold of earthly wisdom.

That interpretation may be helpful to some people; it might even inspire you. But when you look at the text, Jesus is not talking about wisdom; he's talking about gold or silver or money, and he's saying, "Don't take it along." When Francis reads the text, he does not try to find another kind of meaning, but rather, he takes it to mean real gold, silver, or money. He is not an allegorist; he is one who seeks the literal meaning of the text—what the words really mean, what the author was trying to get across by the words that were being used.

Let's contrast that with the next principle: *realistic*. I have yoked the two words together, *literal* and *realistic*. I do that in order to bring out the idea that, while Francis did become very literal in approaching Scripture, he was also realistic. He was not literalistic. He was not fundamentalist. He was not mechanistic, if you will. He did take the words for what they meant, but then he also used the guidance of the Spirit and his own human intelligence guided by grace to appreciate what these words should really mean.

So how does this work? The Scripture text says to take along only one tunic. When Francis finally gives his Rule, he tells his friars, "You can have one tunic, but those who wish can have another one." There's also the part where Jesus tells the disciples they should not wear shoes. Francis says in case of necessity, wear shoes. He does tell his friars not to wear them, but in case of necessity they may do so. And in other places in the Rule, Francis says, "And if at any time because of climate and so on, the ministers decide that the clothing should be somewhat different, go ahead and make such decisions with the blessing of God."[18]

In approaching Scripture, Francis does not say, "Everyone, every time, no matter what the circumstances will always have to do it like this." He's realistic. He's seeing that in certain circumstances you don't need to take things that literally. Be literal, yes, but in a realistic way; that is why I put the two words closely together. I'm talking very much about the same ideas in both of these, but I'm trying to get across very clearly that while he could be very literal, Francis was not a fundamentalist.

One of the best examples of a fundamentalist might be this: If you read the opening chapters of Genesis, you see that God made the world in six days and then he rested. A literalist, a fundamentalist, will insist that God made the world in six twenty-four-hour periods, then he sat down and rested. That's taking the text beyond being merely literal. It's not realistic. That's not seeing what the text is really driving at. Francis had the good sense not to be caught in that literal kind of approach; rather, he took a literal and realistic approach.

Another interesting little item is this: people will often say, "See how literally Francis took the text?" And I will say, "Yes, but notice how he does modify it." We see this not only in the examples mentioned before, but there's another part of the same story, Matthew 10:7–10. It has been said that, when Francis heard this Gospel read at Mass, he was wearing a belt. Well, afterward he got rid of the belt and put a cord around him. The text says nothing about that, and yet he did it on the occasion of hearing that text.

Why? What this is pointing to, what I'm trying to get at, is that Francis was approaching the real meaning of the text, which was something more like this: "God wants me to preach the kingdom of God. Nothing else should distract me, nothing else should distract anybody else who is hearing me. I shouldn't be overly concerned about what I wear. I shouldn't take care of my own comfort. The important thing is, God wants me to preach the Gospel to the poor, so I will forget everything else. By the way I live and the way I am as I preach, I will show them what the Gospel is all about."

Francis sees that this is what Jesus is driving at when he addresses his disciples, and that's what he himself is driving at when he takes this text and applies it to himself. This business about the belt he was wearing? That was the garb of a hermit in those days, and probably what Francis had in mind was that a hermit had a certain status in the Church. Francis didn't want any status in the Church, and so he took a woolen cord and put that around him because that's the way the poor people of his day wore their clothing. Then he was able to go forth and have no concern for anything else except preaching the kingdom of God. His word said that and his garments said that.

The next two words are *personal* and *practical*. Again, I see these as fitting closely together; they really somewhat overlap with *realistic*, as well. I'd like to tell a couple little stories here that may be helpful.

A certain six-year-old boy and his family had the practice of reading the Scriptures together. One evening they were reading the account of Jesus overturning the tables of the merchants in the temple (see John 2:13–17). After the whole text was read the parents asked the children, "What is going on here? What does this story mean?" The children all noticed that Jesus was angry when he was casting out these money changers, and so the next question was, "Why do you think he was angry? Why did he do this?"

Each of the children gave an answer as best they could, and when they came to the six-year-old boy he said, "Jesus was crabby." The mother stopped and tried to figure out, "What is he talking about, Jesus was crabby? What kind of an explanation is this?" And so she said to her son, "Why are you saying that?" The boy replied, "Well, when he was on his way to the Temple, he saw that fig tree, and it didn't have any fruit on it, and he was hungry. He went up to it, and he didn't get any fruit so he was angry. He was crabby because he didn't have anything to eat." See, the boy was looking at himself and looking at the text in that light. He knew that when he didn't get anything to eat when he was hungry he got crabby, and so Jesus would also.

Here's another little story about that same little boy; in fact, it might have taken place the next day. The little boy went to church with his mother, and because he's six years old, he's beginning to read. He looks up and sees a banner up in front near the altar, and he begins to figure out the letters, trying to understand what that banner says. Finally, he gets it, and he taps his mother and says, "Does that banner say, 'Jesus loves sinners'?" And she says, "Yes, that's right." Then he yanks on her again, "Is that really true?" "Yes, it's true; now please be quiet." "But then why do you always tell me to be good?"

Again, this little boy sees the text in terms of himself, how he felt and what his experiences were. That's the point I want to make by these stories. In the second story, we see that the boy is pretty good at making the words apply to himself, but he stopped a little soon. Maybe he just hasn't had enough experience yet to appreciate what the statement "Jesus loves sinners" might mean. If we try to understand that phrase, we would surely go to the next step and see that this is not saying we should go ahead and be sinners, but we can't help that we have been sinners. This is our consolation.

We know that God loves us, that Jesus loves us, and so we do not need to despair. Then we might even take the next step that this phrase suggests: If Jesus loves sinners, then we are called to love sinners. That would be a fairly full understanding of the text. With this in mind we can go and apply it to our lives, our personal relationships, our approach to the world, and so on.

These two stories show us something of what a personal approach to Scripture is all about. We all need to have some of the simple intuition of a child.

When Francis heard the passage from Matthew at Mass that day, right away he seemed to have come to an understanding of how that text applied to himself.

He saw how it fit with some of his ideals and challenged others; he believed it was leading him to stir up his life some more. We can learn from Francis that we, too, should let Scripture stir something up inside us. Let it be a real challenge to come out of ourselves.

Another way to consider this principle of seeing the Word as personal is this: We don't interpret the text; the text interprets us. And that's where the little boy was wrong. It was nice that he became so personal in his understanding of the words, but he interpreted them according to his own restricted view. What an adult should do and can do, an adult in Christ, is see that the text is telling us to do something about who we are and how we live and what our vision of life might be. That, I suggest, is really making the text personal.

Taking this one step further, by *personal* I really do not mean that it should just be an individualistic thing. Francis applied the Gospel to himself as an individual person, but his whole life was caught up in the Church and in the needs of the world. He saw himself as a member of that world and therefore, he was called to deal with that world at large. And so *personal* does not mean *individualistic*. It means applying the text to me in the context of my whole world.

Let's take a closer look at the word *practical*. What I've said about *personal* already is in the direction of practical. By *practical*, I don't mean *pragmatic*, meaning how we'll use something, or we'll appreciate something and make use of it if it can do something for us. If we can get some money out of something or glory—that's the American way of approaching pragmatism. We don't care what ultimate value is inherent there; all we are trying to see is what we can get out of it. That would be pragmatic.

Practical means that something affects me in way that changes me, that gets me going. If it's practical, it gets me to do something. The Scripture text from Matthew prompted Francis to make a change in his clothing and encouraged his idea to go out and announce the Gospel, proclaiming the kingdom of God and inviting everyone to penance.

Here's an example of this. One day a few of us were making a big crock of spaghetti sauce—really big, maybe ten gallons or so. And as we were lifting it from one place to another, guess what happened? The crock dropped and broke, and spaghetti sauce began oozing all over the place. There we stood ready to cry—literally!—as we watched the sauce going down in between the cracks of the tile. We were having visions of the whole floor falling in. Well, we must have been in a bit of shock because we just stood there and watched the sauce start oozing toward the door, right toward the nice new carpet that had just been put down in the next room. Fortunately, one of the priests in charge came by just then, and spoke sharply: "Don't just stand there. Do something!" So we ran and found some mops and buckets and started cleaning up the mess before it became worse.

That's what Francis did. He didn't just stand there; he did something. That's what I mean by practical. It suggests that this is the way that we might approach a text. Each time we hear a text, can we not make the words our own? Yes, this is what I wish, this is what I seek, this is what I long for with all my heart; then go ahead and do something about it. That's what Francis did; he made the text practical.

Here's another way of coming to a practical perspective. When you read a text, first hear the proclamation, then answer the call. This is a good way of interpreting many texts. Hear the proclamation, answer the call. In the case of Francis, what is the proclamation Jesus is giving through the text? He's saying the kingdom of God is important: I want you to announce the kingdom of God, and that is so important I want you to get rid of all the stuff that gets in the way, even your clothing. Be simple; be poor so that people know you believe in the kingdom of God. That's the proclamation Francis hears.

What is the call, then? The call is to do something about it. Change your ways, change your clothing, get on the road and announce the kingdom of God. Hear the proclamation, and answer the call. It's a helpful way of getting at what's really both personal and practical.

The last principle is *spiritual*. The word stands there all by itself, yet it really is connected with everything else. In the two previous chapters, I've done a lot of explanation of the word *spiritual*." The words that we have in the Scriptures are Spirit and life, especially the words we have in the Gospel. If these words, then, are Spirit and life and the Holy Spirit dwells within us, we need to have a spiritual approach.

I'm not using the word *spiritual* in opposition to *material*; rather, I'm using it to apply to the Spirit of God in the text and in our hearts. God wants us to appreciate everything he has made, and so we certainly want to appreciate the material things of this world. When I use the word *spiritual*, I am stressing the place of the Spirit of God in our approach to Scripture.

By *spiritual*, I mean that we get beyond the words to God. Where is God in this text? What is God saying to me? What does he want of me? How is he relating to me through the words of this text? The important thing is not to get all caught up in the details of the text. So even as I said Francis is literal, I also said he's realistic. He looks at what the words really mean; indeed, those words have meaning insofar as the Spirit of God is talking to us through them. Somehow, God himself is coming into our lives through those words.

If we get bogged down in arguing about whether we're going to wear one coat or two coats, whether we're going to wear shoes or sandals or go barefoot; if we spend our time worrying about wearing a belt or a cord, then we're missing the point. Those things are important only insofar as they signify some-thing else. God is telling Francis, "I can make myself known to you, and then through you to others, if you make clothing and a lot of other material concerns secondary. Put them where they belong. I want to come into your life."

That's what I'm trying to say about a spiritual perspective: Get beyond the words to God. Don't make even the words of Scripture an idol. They are not meant to be worshipped as such. They are meant to lead us to God.

There are some people who play what I call "Scripture Bingo." They throw phrases at you such as John 3:16, "God so loved the world that he gave his only Son" and in 1 John 4:16, "God is love," but what good does it do? That's not getting to the God behind the words; that's playing a game.

Another way to appreciate what I mean by *spiritual* is simply to repeat what I have said before: Francis comes to Scripture out of prayer. We need to pray because it is in prayer that we come into contact with God. It is in prayer that the Holy Spirit can get hold of us. It is in prayer that we finally open up so that God can really get in and do something in our lives.

Another word I would connect with the spiritual approach is *mystery*. A few years back the United States Catholic Conference of Bishops issued a statement that advised priests to take a mystery approach to preaching. The bishops said that a priest should first discover in the text the mystery that's present there. What is the mystery of God that is especially evident in this text? For example, in Paul's Letter to the Romans, there are constant references to faith, and so we might say that the mystery of faith is very strong in those readings. Or in many of the lectionary texts, the theme of prayer is very strong, and we might see there the mystery of God's relation to us and our relation to God.

To continue on in the case of preaching, the first thing a priest might do is get at the mystery that is there, and the next thing is to help people see where it fits into their lives. So if you're talking about the relationship of God to us in prayer—if that's the mystery we discover in the text—then we might preach about how to pray better. We might look at the text realistically and say, for example, how do you talk about prayer to people who work hard all day, then come home exhausted, too tired to even think? How do they pray? It's up to the priest to help people see that even in a situation such as this the mystery of prayer can be realized. The mystery of God's relationship to people can be made real.

We can take this mystery approach and use it as another way of getting at the spiritual meaning of a text. As you read a text you might ask, "What is the mystery here?" In Matthew 10:7–10, which we've been referring to throughout this chapter, the mystery of the kingdom of God is evident there. Here is the mystery of God's conquering love of all creation, God's invincible love that is always effective and has been effective from the very first moment of creation to the end.

In this text Francis hears Jesus telling him, "This is the way you can respond to this Gospel: by the way you live, and then as you go out as a minister of the Gospel." So the mystery is the kingdom of God, and the next step is to think about how you might put that into practice by the way you live. The answer is in the text somehow. As we try to apply this to our own situation, we can come up with a greater appreciation of what God may be telling each of us in our own daily struggles in life.

You may be familiar with the poetry of Gerard Manley Hopkins. Even though he was a Jesuit, he was very much influenced by John Duns Scotus, who was a great Franciscan, and Hopkins has an approach to created reality that conforms well to our own. In his poem "God's Grandeur," he begins with these words: "The world is charged with the grandeur of God." I think those words can also be used for Scripture.

The Word of God in Scripture is charged with the grandeur of God. If we have a real spiritual approach to Scripture, we will begin to appreciate the grandeur that is there. By *grandeur* I mean not only the awesome aspect of God, most holy and high and supreme, but also God the humble, the simple. For instance, look at the parable of the widow harassing the judge, going back to him over and over again, saying, "I want my rights" (see Luke 18:1–8). Finally, the judge gives in because he can't take it anymore; that's a pretty funny story, I think. It can help us appreciate something of God's down-to-earthiness. So the Word of God is charged with the grandeur of God—all the grandeur of God, even that simple grandeur of God's humor.

In that same poem, Hopkins also writes that in nature "There lives the dearest freshness deep down things," a very beautiful expression. Applying that directly to Scripture, there, too, lives the dearest freshness deep down things. If we sense the spirit of God in the Word and approach it with a spiritual heart, we will discover something of that very dear freshness of God that's deep in those words. This is a spiritual approach.

The English mystic and poet William Blake has this statement, and again I think it so nicely can apply to this spiritual approach. In his poem "The Marriage of Heaven and Hell" he writes, "If the doors of perception were cleansed, everything would appear to man as it is: infinite." Blake is talking about the world, that if we could really see with cleansed perception, we would see infinity. The same goes for Scripture. If we can really cleanse our perception, get beyond the words themselves, we will begin to experience the One who is deeply embedded in the Scripture—that is, God.

My suggestion, then, is to approach Scripture by using the five principles, or words, that guided Francis: *literal, realistic, personal, practical, spiritual.* You don't have to make everything fit in each one of those categories, just use them as a guideline. When you read a text you might say, "What am I going to do with this?" And so you might look at it and ask, "What's the realistic meaning here?" or "What do these words really say to me, and what should I do about it?"

Recall the three texts that Francis read when he went to the Church of St. Nicholas with Brother Bernard, and opened the Bible three times. The order in which the texts appeared is Matthew 19:21, then Luke 9:3, and then Matthew 16:24. If you look at them in that order you see that the first text says to get rid of everything. The second one says not to take anything along for the journey. And the third one says simply, "Follow me." It's a rather nice progression as given in Bonaventure's account of Francis's life.[19]

Let's go back to the first text they found: "If you will be perfect, go, sell all that you have and give to the poor"; that's what is quoted in Bonaventure, just those words. That doesn't mean they ignored the other words in the passage from Matthew, but those are the words that are singled out. If we try to approach this in a literal and realistic way, we see that Jesus is talking about the possibility of being perfect: This is the way we can be perfect.

But now let's take it a step further to see what more Jesus might mean by that. Maybe the best insight into these words is a phrase from the Sermon on the Mount, when Jesus tells his disciples, "Be perfect, therefore, as your heavenly Father is perfect" (Matthew 5:48). As we saw earlier, this means that, as God sends his gifts on both the good and bad, so we are called to do the same. We don't hold back anything from someone in need. We don't question first whether they are worthy or not, but rather, accept that they are human beings who are our brothers and sisters under God. Therefore, just as God is perfect in giving what is needed to his children, so we are called to be perfect in that same way. Of course, that is an awfully tall order!

It's easy to be generous when a nice person comes along. Look at Mother Teresa. People were exceedingly generous to her; people did many things for her because she was easily lovable. But look at the people she took care of. She picked them up out of the gutter every day, dirty and smelling and diseased and practically dead, and she loved them and took care of them without question. For most of us, it's a lot easier to love Mother Teresa but not as easy to love the people whom she cared for.

But we're not called to go to India and do that kind of thing; maybe we're not even called to do that kind of work in our own corner of the world. Maybe we are called to be perfect simply by helping the people around us. Maybe we are called to forgive, to let bygones be bygones. Do we only care about people who are nice to us, or do we care about the people who are not nice to us at all?

Being perfect doesn't necessarily mean we have to treat everybody well, be nice to everybody. That's not what God is. God isn't just nice to everybody; God gives himself to everybody. In this same way every person that comes into my life is saying to me, "Get out of yourself; don't hang on to your own selfish concerns. Don't put your own concerns so far above everybody else's that you don't care about anybody else." Let people into your life; that's one way you can start trying to be perfect.

But in Matthew 19:21, Jesus does indicate further ramifications of being perfect. If you really want to be like your heavenly Father, if you really want to go all out for him and be like him, go sell your possessions and give to the poor. Now here's where Francis gives us a good insight in this text. He and Bernard and the brothers and sisters who will eventually follow Francis do indeed take this text literally and realistically. Franciscans go back home, get all their possessions together, sell them, give the money to the poor, and then come to follow him.

How does this help secular Franciscans, or those who don't specifically follow a Franciscan lifestyle? Francis was faced with that problem as well. People came to him and said, "We want to follow you; we want to be like to you." Some of them wanted to leave their wives and their families; there were even wives who wanted to leave their husbands and their families. Francis was realistic enough to know that leaving everything behind was not the right way for everybody.

Here we might recall the story about Franz Jägerstätter, who finally had to go to this extreme when it came to making a choice to be faithful to God or not. Then, for all practical purposes, he did have to give up everything. He could not put the love of his wife and his children ahead of his love for God; that's the way it came to him. This is a good way of understanding Matthew's text for people who don't enter a religious community.

People who are living with their families or as a single person or in some other situation can still leave everything behind in the sense that they will never put material possessions—even one's family or relationships with others—above their fidelity to God. If that is the way they live, they are exemplifying the kingdom of God. They are, as the rest of the text says, storing up treasure in heaven. Remember, *heaven* stands for God. A person who puts God first has treasure with God, is with God. Possess God and you will be possessed by God.

Surely, then they are following Christ. So to apply this text in a very practical and realistic way is to say, "Put possessions in their right place. Don't hang onto anything; get rid of stuff as much as you can." Material possessions are unimportant as far as the kingdom of God is concerned. Of course, there are things that we need to live, to do our work, to help us relax, and to be better people. But when possessions get in the way of our relationship with God, that's when we need to consider what needs to go.

Another question is, "What does poverty mean for a layperson? What is the practical implication of this kind of vow in someone's life?" It means they become detached from things. They come to use material goods for their own needs, for the needs of their family, and for other legitimate purposes. There are differences of opinion about how you really carry this out. Essentially, however, to take a vow of poverty—or to ascribe to that way of life without actually taking a vow—means we cannot cling to anything. When we cling to our possessions, for all practical purposes we renounce Christ. If we must make a choice between renouncing Christ or renouncing goods, we have to renounce goods. Christ must be first, foremost, and everything in our lives.

Sometimes the choice between possessions and Christ can be a dramatic thing; more often it occurs in the daily choices of our lives. For example, how do we deal with consumerism? How much do we need to hang onto? How important is it for us to keep getting new things, getting the best things, getting ahead of everybody else? Surely we are called to use our possessions well and become good stewards of whatever we have. That especially includes taking care of the poor.

Each situation in life challenges us to consider the words of Scripture in a practical, realistic, and personal way; that's why we never want to stop reading Scripture, and hearing its words proclaimed to us at Mass. Each time we encounter Scripture, it offers an opportunity to consider the choices we have before us as followers of Christ.

Going back to Franz Jägerstätter, I'm not condemning every other Austrian for not doing what

Jägerstätter did. But he came to the point where he said, "God is calling me to say no to these people who are trying to take me into their army and fight for their cause. I don't believe in their cause. It's against Christ, and I can't go that way." And so he took the words of God very personally and practically and carried them out that way. Other people found different ways of looking at their possessions and their lives, and shuffled their priorities in such a way they didn't need to make such a radical choice. Maybe there were others who, like Jägerstätter, were faithful to their beliefs and made similar choices, or changed their minds.

Each Scripture text is a call to try to understand that text as it stands, consider what it is saying to you, and then remain open to the possibilities suggested by the text.

We spent a good deal of time with Luke 9:3 in a previous chapter, "Take nothing for the journey." Take neither walking staff nor traveling bag, no bread, no money; no one is to have two coats. This again is a good illustration of the virtue of poverty.

The third text in Bonaventure's account, Matthew 16:24, tells us "If you have a mind to come my way, renounce yourself, and take up your cross and follow me."[20] In this text the really important words are the last ones: "Follow me." If we understand that and can make it real in our lives, the rest of these things may follow. But how are we to follow in the footsteps of Christ?

What does this mean practically and realistically? What does it mean personally? How literally do we take those words? And if we don't take them literally, what do those words mean to say?

Following in the footsteps of Christ doesn't mean that we should all go over to the Holy Land, try to find the footsteps of Jesus, and walk in them. It means, rather, that our lives must become identified with the life of Christ. We should approach life the way he approached life. If it means carrying the cross, whatever that implies in our modern age and in our own personal circumstances, that is what we must do.

We might well ask ourselves, why was Jesus put to death? He was put to death because he was faithful to his Father. He did what was asked of him by God the Father; nobody wanted to hear about that, especially the people in power, both civil and religious. None of them wanted to hear what Jesus had to say. Today we're tempted to do the same; we don't want to hear about what my Father wants us to do because we're afraid of the consequences. What might it do to us? How would we have to change? But Jesus decided, "I will do what God wants, no matter what." In challenging the people of his day, the civil and the religious authorities, he gradually came to realize he would even lose his life because of fidelity to his Father.

Be Faithful

Look at your life. Where are you really being faithful? How can you be more faithful? It's easy to be faithful in some things. For most of us, it's just some rather small things that demand fidelity; still, we give up on it. For example, look at the times when we'll get in a little bit of trouble unless we tell a lie. This lie probably isn't serious, and we should have a few faults anyway, so we tell a lie and that solves a lot of problems for us. Yet, maybe that's exactly when we're called to be faithful. We won't end up being put on a cross or sent to the guillotine or something drastic like that, but telling the truth will cause us some trouble—and we'd rather avoid trouble.

Christ says, "If you want to come after me, really follow in my footsteps, be faithful as I was faithful to the Father." That means all those little compromises that are so easy for us to make must go: a lie here, a little cheating there, a little bit of backbiting over there. All these things can make life easier for us, but Christ is calling us to be faithful in all of these things, to really follow in his footsteps and be faithful to his Father.

Whether it's big things or small things, Jesus makes a very strong statement here: If anyone wishes to follow after him, that person needs to deny his very self. Deny his very self. Does that mean we shouldn't be selfish; is that what it literally means? Surely, it means at least that: to get over that selfishness that wants to keep protecting the self, to stop making compromises, to stop allowing ourselves to be indifferent.

But it means even more than that because Jesus doesn't say, "Deny your selfishness"; he says to deny yourself. Now, we know that God made us and that we are a treasured part of creation; God doesn't want us to destroy ourselves. But what is it that's being asked of us when we are told to deny ourselves? Does this mean we should see that God has to be most important in our lives, that we must be secondary to God? Maybe that's a bad way of putting it, too. God is all important; God is everything. And whenever we compromise, even in the smallest way, by putting ourselves before God and before others, those are the times when we do not deny ourselves. And so while we must give up our attachment to possessions and give to the poor, we must also give up our very selves and realize that God is first; Jesus is first.

And so we are called to deny ourselves, to take up whatever cross there is in our lives, whatever kind of pain comes into our lives, and really begin to follow in Christ's footsteps. Francis sums up this well in his simple, little prayer: "My God and my all."

CHAPTER FOUR

How Francis Lived in the Gospel Light

O great and glorious God and my Lord Jesus Christ, send your Spirit into our midst that he may enlighten our minds and inflame our hearts, that he may give us a right faith, a certain hope, and a perfect charity. In this way, through this Spirit, we pray that we may be able to understand the Word of God given to us in the Scriptures by the Holy Spirit, and that as he dwells in our hearts, he may bring us closer to you and closer to all our brothers and sisters in the world today. We ask that you hear this prayer and grant it through Christ our Lord. Amen.

*F*rancis's love for Scripture is part of his love for the Church and for the sacraments. He came to Scripture with a deep sense of prayer, led by the Spirit who he knew lived within him and who was speaking to him from the Word of God. From this, he formed his principles of interpreting Scripture, summed up in five words: *literal, realistic, personal, practical,* and *spiritual.*

Now we'll take the next step and look at how Francis lived out the Gospel, and how living a Gospel life emerged from his understanding of Scripture. We know that his adoption of a Gospel life was due to many factors—his early training, his mother assuredly, his schooling, what he received from the Church, both the official Church and all other members of the Church. But there was also a very important contribution that came from the Scriptures themselves and the way he understood them.

Let's first look at a little story. Ramakrishna was a mystic who lived in India over a hundred years ago. One day, as he was walking through the marketplace, he saw a servant boy being whipped by his master. As he watched that boy being whipped, welts appeared on Ramakrishna's own body. This suggests that this man had such a strong feeling for this boy that he could identify with him in the sufferings that he was enduring. I like to use this story as a modern counterpart, because it is a hundred years old and takes place in another part of the world, coming out of a different situation, a different culture from our own, from the Bible, and from Francis.

In contrast, I refer to the third consideration of the stigmata of St. Francis, an account of which is found in "The Little Flowers of St. Francis."[21] Imagine here a parallel between Ramakrishna and Francis. It is the Feast of the Cross, September 14. Some time before dawn Francis began to pray outside the entrance of his cell. Turning his face toward the East, he prayed in this way:

> My Lord Jesus Christ, I pray You to grant me two graces before I die: the first is that during my life I may feel in my soul and in my body, as much as possible, that pain which You, dear Jesus, sustained in the hour of Your most bitter Passion. The second is that I may feel in my heart, as much as possible, that excessive love with which You, O Son of God, were inflamed in willingly enduring such suffering for us sinners.
>
> And remaining for a long time in that prayer he understood that God would grant it

to him, and that it would soon be conceded to him to feel those things as much as is possible for a mere creature.

Having received this promise, St. Francis began to contemplate with intense devotion the Passion of Christ and his infinite charity. And the fervor of his devotion increased so much within him that he utterly transformed himself into Jesus through love and compassion. And while he was thus inflaming himself in this contemplation, on that same morning he saw coming down from Heaven a Seraph with six resplendent and flaming wings. As the Seraph, flying swiftly, came closer to St. Francis, so that he could perceive him clearly, he noticed that He had the likeness of a Crucified Man, and his wings were so disposed that two wings extended above his head, two were spread out to fly, and the other two covered his entire body.

On seeing this St. Francis was very much afraid, and at the same time he was filled with joy and grief and amazement. He felt intense joy from the friendly look of Christ, who appeared to him in a very familiar way and gazed at him very kindly. But on the other hand, seeing him nailed to the Cross, he felt boundless grief and compassion. Next, he was greatly amazed at such an astounding and extraordinary vision, for he knew well that the affliction of suffering is not in accord with the immortality of the angelic Seraph. And while he was marveling thus, He who was appearing to him revealed to him that this vision was shown to him by Divine Providence in this particular form in order that he should understand that he was to be utterly transformed into the direct likeness of Christ Crucified, not by physical martyrdom, but by enkindling of the mind....

Now when, after a long time and a secret conversation, this wonderful vision disappeared, it left a most intense ardor and flame of divine love in the heart of St. Francis, and it left a marvelous image and imprint of the Passion of Christ in his flesh. For soon there began to appear in the hands and feet of St. Francis the marks of nails such as he had just seen in the body of Jesus Crucified, who had appeared to him in the form of a Seraph. For his hands and feet seemed to be pierced through the center with nails, the heads of which were in the palms of his hands and in the upper part of his feet outside the flesh, and their points extended through the back of the hands and the soles of the feet so far that they seemed to be bent and beaten back in such a way that underneath their bent and beaten-back point—all of which stood out from the flesh—it would have been easy to put the finger of one's hand as through a ring. And the heads of the nails were round and black. Likewise in his right side appeared the wound of a blow from a spear, which was open, red, and bloody, and from which blood often issued from the holy breast of St. Francis and stained his habit and breeches.[22]

This story tells of how Francis prayed to feel in his body something of Jesus's pain, and in his heart something of his love. We are not really sure what Francis said on this occasion, rather, the writer cited in the *Omnibus* is putting words in the mouth of Francis that will dramatize and help us understand something of what was going on in Francis's own mind and heart. We might say the writer saw the wounds that Francis received and then was able to infer what the sentiments of Francis really were.

If you look at this scene and compare it with the story about Ramakrishna, you'll see that something of the same thing happened. Surely we would say that what happened to Francis can be called a miracle. But we can also say that, in a way, it was the most natural thing in the world to happen because he had become so united with Christ crucified.

This had been the story of his life. Since his conversion some eighteen years earlier, he continually had grown more and more into the image of Christ crucified. He so identified with the sufferings of Christ that the marks of that suffering found their way onto his hands and his feet and his side, and into his heart. And not only the sufferings but also a mysterious love of God and that love of the human Jesus as well that desired to save the world, that did become so real to Francis that it's the most natural thing in the world that it would find its external expression upon him. Like Ramakrishna, who was so at one with God that he could walk through the marketplace and become one with God's creations, especially this poor servant, Francis so identified with the suffering of Jesus that he took on the wounds himself.

I would suggest that all of Francis's experiences, and in a particular way his involvement with the Word of God in Scripture, led him to such a point that he was identified with Christ crucified. To see how this evolved, we can go to some of Francis's writings and see if there is something there that might help us understand his approach to Scripture, and act as the background on which we can understand his love for Christ and his identification with Christ crucified.

In the Letter to All the Faithful, Francis tells us that "those who love God are happy and blessed. They do as our Lord himself tells us in the Gospel, "Thou shalt love the Lord they God with they whole heart, and with thy whole soul,...and thy neighbor as thyself."[23]

Francis goes on to say that this is what you do when you love God and your neighbor. You don't indulge in vices and sins, but love God, yourself, and others. Furthermore, you receive the body and blood of our Lord Jesus Christ." So we notice right away how Christian life, Christian living, is closely connected with the Eucharist. This is very important in Francis's mind, because then you go on to produce worthy fruits of penance.

We might even add here Luke 3:8, "Bear fruits worthy of repentance." You receive the Eucharist, and then out of the strength received in that sacrament, Jesus brings about change from a life of selfishness and sin to a life of doing penance. Penance does not necessarily mean doing difficult things, but it means changing from a selfish viewpoint to living for God, repenting. The way we live will show that we are repenting.

If you are making an effort to live a Christian life, if you are receiving the Eucharist and allowing that to have its power in your life, surely the Spirit of the Lord will rest upon you. He will make his home and dwelling among you. The Spirit of God will live among the group that does penance and surely within each person who does penance.

"These people who have the Spirit dwelling among them, are children of the Heavenly Father." This comes right out of Matthew 5:45. "They will be children of your Father in heaven, whose work they do. It is they who are the brides, the brothers and the mothers of our Lord Jesus Christ," refers to Matthew 12:50.

Here is the text so we know exactly where Francis is coming from; I will begin a few verses earlier to set the whole scene:

> While he was still speaking to the crowds, his mother and his brothers were standing outside, wanting to speak to him. Someone told him, "Look, your mother and your brothers are standing outside, wanting to speak to you." But to the one who had told him this, Jesus replied, "Who is my mother,

and who are my brothers?" And pointing to his disciples, he said, "Here are my mother and my brothers! For whoever does the will of my Father in heaven is my brother and sister and mother." (Matthew 12:46–50)

Going back to Francis's quotation, you'll notice there is one thing that Francis adds to this quotation: the word *brides*.[24] In the First Letter to Agnes of Prague, Clare uses the text from Matthew in the same way, adding the word *spouse*. I think Clare was picking up on something Francis himself first uttered, in adding the word *spouse* to Matthew 12:50. We don't know for sure, but it really doesn't matter. The important thing is that he did use the word *brides*, and this is critical to understanding how Francis envisions Christian living.

Heart of Christian Living

Now we get into the heart of Francis's vision of Christian living. The Letter to All the Faithful helps us see the very roots of Francis's Gospel living and his relationship to Christ, as well as to the Father and the Holy Spirit. Francis offers a kind of commentary on this text.

First he defines his use of the word *brides*: "A person is his bride when his faithful soul is united with Jesus

Christ by the Holy Spirit." A bit further, Francis picks up on that theme: "How glorious it is, how holy and wonderful it is to have a Father in heaven. How holy it is, how beautiful and lovable it is to have in heaven a Bridegroom." [25] As is typical of his writing, Francis is emoting over the wonder that is settling into his heart as he contemplates his relationship to Jesus. Indeed, he sees Jesus as his spouse.

This brings us right to the heart of Francis's understanding of Christian living, of Gospel living. By adding the word *bride* to the text, he made the Gospel personal to himself. In this, he also becomes creative. He uses his imagination and broadens the reality of what's being said in the Scripture text. He is not restricted just to the words, but he's getting at what the Holy Spirit is suggesting to him in this text. Francis uses the word *bride* in this particular verse in order to bring out what the Holy Spirit is really saying to him.

Spousal love is a popular theme in the Old Testament, especially for the prophets Hosea and Jeremiah. Also, we have the beautiful imagery in the Canticle of Canticles, or Song of Songs, that shows God as the spouse of his people. God loves his people so much that he is the husband and the people his bride. That image, that symbol is meant to suggest something of the tremendous love the God of the Old Testament had for his people. It is a lovely contrast to the image of a powerful, awe-inspiring, even angry God sometimes depicted in the Old Testament.

The whole of the Song of Songs shows human love as God would have it, but it is also interpreted in terms of God's love for his people and the people's love for God. The early Church Fathers and the mystics of the Middle Ages picked up on that theme because it continued what they read in the New Testament, where it says that Jesus is indeed the spouse of the Church. They then expanded this theme to say that, if Jesus is the spouse of the Church, he is indeed the spouse of every member of the Church.

That's what Francis is getting at. He is saying that God's relationship to us in Christ is not just that God did something for us in giving us his Son, and that we should be grateful because eventually, if we're lucky, we'll get to heaven. Rather, he's saying God plunged himself into us, into our lives, through Jesus Christ, who suffered and died on the cross. Through his passion, Jesus enabled us to live the very life of God, so that God really is our Father and he loves us more than any human father or mother, all human parents put together, can love their children. God loves us in Christ and joins us to himself in an intimate way—such an intimate way that by the power of the Holy Spirit, we are one with Christ, and through him children of God, our Father.

Continuing with his Letter, Francis picks up on the other symbols in the text of Matthew. He says, "We are brothers to him, when we do the will of the Father who is in heaven." Again, "We are his brothers and sisters when we do the will of his Father, who is in heaven." We show that we are children of God not simply by wearing his name—by saying we are people who believe in God, or we are Christians, people who believe in Christ. We are brothers and sisters of Christ *when* we do his will and do the will of his Father, even as Christ did.

Again, this is an image, a metaphor if you will, but yet it's telling us about the real relationship we have with God. We truly show that we are brothers and sisters of Jesus when we do what our loving Father wants us to do. This is Francis's understanding of living the Gospel, of following Christ. He is still not finished, because he has another beautiful image. It's rather surprising that Jesus would use it, and yet he did. Francis picks up on it and makes it clear to us, expands it in his way.

Jesus said, "For whoever does the will of my Father in heaven is my brother and sister and mother"

(Matthew 12:50). Francis tells us that "we are mothers to him when we enthrone him in our hearts and souls by love with a pure and sincere conscience, and give him birth by doing good. This too, should be an example to others."[26]

Then because of that closeness, we show that Jesus is within us by having a pure and sincere conscience. Psychologists today might say that we are authentic. We look at ourselves, we look at God, we look at life, and we look at it straight and honestly and make our decisions accordingly. We have a pure and sincere conscience. We don't put on airs, we don't get hypocritical; we admit who and what we really are. In doing that, we show that we are carrying Christ. This is something that we don't bring about on our own; it's the pure gift of divine love.

After carrying Christ in this way, we might say we also then give birth to him through his holy manner of working. In other words, our giving forth Jesus in birth allows him to use us to continue his life on earth so that what we do is his holy manner of working. He is born into the world because we give him ourselves to continue to do his work.

Francis finishes up that verse by noting this holy manner of working should shine before others as an example. Not that we are putting on a front, but rather, we are simply allowing Christ to live in us and work in us. Therefore, naturally, whatever we do will bring light to the world.

Francis goes on to express the depths of his emotion. "How holy and beloved, how pleasing and lowly, how peaceful, delightful, lovable and desirable above all things it is to have a Brother like this, who laid down his life for his sheep (cf. Jn 10:15)."

Francis then recalls how Jesus prayed for his disciples and for us at the Last Supper. He quotes extensively from John 17:6–24. We might interpret Francis as saying that Jesus is praying that those who follow him will live along the lines Francis has already described.

Francis and Our Gospel Life

Our attempts at understanding Francis and what he means to our lives might well be served if we take this prayer of Francis and try to look at it in terms of what it is that Jesus prayed. How is he praying for us? What can that mean to our life? Is his prayer being answered, and can we trust that it is? Maybe we can also learn from this how we might pray for ourselves and for others, and eventually how we might best be like Francis in living a Gospel life.

Ramakrishna saw a boy beaten, and felt that in himself. Francis saw Jesus beaten, hanging on the cross, and felt that in his own life. Francis built up to that point through a life of looking at Jesus, growing in love for him, making him his spouse, his brother, and even his child. Through Jesus, then, he reached out to the world and made the world one with himself. In fact, is that not why Francis refers to the prayer of Jesus in the Gospel of John—"Holy Father, in your name keep those you have given me… so that they may be sanctified in unity, just as we are" (17:11)—praying that they may be one as Jesus made himself one with the world? Francis made himself one with Jesus and also made himself one with his world.

Francis is not only someone who became a saint and saved his own soul, but also one who was totally involved with God. Through this and through Christ crucified, he embraced the world at large even as Jesus did. Francis became a mystic. Maybe we fear that word. But Francis is telling us, both in his writings and in his life, that we are all called to be mystics. Every Catholic, every Christian, every human being is called to be a mystic. We are to be one with our Father in Jesus by the Spirit and then embrace all of the world, all human beings, and all creation: That's what a mystic does. A mystic has an experience of God, then begins to realize what life is all about.

Since a mystic is one who experiences God, he or she knows that life is meant to be union with God and union with everything else that is of value to God. And if God created this world, everything he made belongs to him. If we belong to God, everything in this world belongs to us. We are called to be mystics by embracing God, and through him, embracing the world at large. This has tremendous ramifications for everything that's going on in our world today, whether it's our own private world, our family world, our neighborhood, our nation, or international affairs. That's the way Francis saw his life, and he sums it all up very beautifully in what I would call the shortest love song ever written: "My God and my all."

In chapter one of the Letter to all the Faithful, there are many references to Scripture. I hope these have been brought into focus by suggesting that each of these Scripture passages shows how we are plunged into the mystery of God. Further, they illustrate in the very real way that God is our Father and that our lives are joined intimately to Jesus; all this is by the power of the Spirit.

But that is still not the full story. In fact, that would be the upshot of Jesus's prayer for his disciples, that he's asking not only that they might be one with himself and his Father, but that they may be one with one another. Francis is saying we will really live the Gospel only when what God is doing in us overflows to those around us, into the world at large. That's one of the reasons why I like that little story about Ramakrishna; his love flowed out from him so strongly and concretely to that very boy who was being whipped that day.

Ramakrishna was a mystic. He was one with God, but he was also one with his world—especially with a person who was suffering. In suggesting that we are all called to be mystics, I am saying that we too should be one with God and thereby become one with everyone else. One area where we can apply this to our world today is the Respect for Life movement. Maybe we think of the aborted child as a real victim of society. I would like to say that Francis is telling us we are one with that child. It's not just that some evil is being done to someone out there; that evil is touching us. We are one with that child; as that baby is killed, so are we being killed.

Let's take that one step further, to the mother who goes through the agony of deciding whether or not to have that abortion. We are one with that person, and so the first thing we must do is not condemn but understand; embrace, even. This means not just understanding with the mind but also with our heart. Likewise, the abortionists, those who promote abortion whether by performing them or by supporting the right to have one: We belong to these people, and they belong to us. We are called to be one with them.

Many of us want to know: "How are we going to save the world? How can we change things?" What Scripture says, what Francis says, is that this will happen when we really become what God has called us to be: mystics. We should not be afraid of that word. It doesn't mean somebody who flies around in the air; it doesn't mean someone who works all kinds of miracles; it doesn't mean you have to be good at healing or even speaking in tongues—although you might be. What it means is that you're one with God. You become God's arms as he reaches out to embrace his world.

Getting back to those who promote abortion: Somehow or other I am one with them. God wants to embrace them. He wants to use me to be part of that embrace. There are abortionists who are sincere, and there are abortionists who are doing it simply to make money; many of us fear that profit might be the biggest motivation for many abortion providers. But even if that's true, God wants us to embrace them, or at least embrace whatever part of their world we really can.

If we look at all the areas where mystics are needed, well, we can't do it all. Even if we can't get directly involved in the movement to protect the lives of unborn children, we can still have a word of encouragement for those who do. We can also have an open heart to those who have had an abortion, as well as to those who perform abortions or support abortion rights, and try to really understand them. Remember, we are the arms of God in this world.

This, of course, applies to other situations as well. St. John Vianney, the Curé of Ars, who lived in France in the nineteenth century, is famous for being a tremendous confessor. Once he became established as a pastor in rural France, he spent anywhere from ten to eighteen hours in the confessional every day of his life. People flocked to him, and he was able to really hear them and understand them and love them. That's what came through in his approach to people. It has been suggested—and St. John might have said it himself—that the reason he was able to have such an impact on penitents was that he was convinced that he himself was capable of doing everything they confessed to him. He could so identify with his penitent that he would never condemn them; rather, he would understand them, and he would love them.

With this in mind, should I condemn abortionists? No, because I could be one of them. Should I condemn even those who are doing it for money? No, because I could be one. The more I can really see that and become one with that person, maybe I will be able to touch them—or rather, God will use me to touch them.

By the way, St. John Vianney was also a member of the secular Franciscans, as well as being a diocesan priest. Anyway, you see where I'm going in all of this. The only people that are going to save the world are not the great philosophers or theologians or scientists or technologists or politicians or economists or anything else; it can only be the people who are one with God.

In this same light, it's been said that Dag Hammarskjöld, Secretary General of the U.N. from 1953 to 1961, was such an outstanding statesman because he was first of all a mystic. It seems to be the case that he was. All this leads to what Francis discovered: He wanted to be one with Christ, and in being one with Christ, he embraced the whole world. This included not only human beings but all of creation. The mystic loves all of creation and is one with it. In his very beautiful Canticle of the Creatures, Francis illustrates his all-embracing love of creation and unfolds his basic attitude of what it means to live the Gospel.

One who lives the Gospel embraces the world. One who lives the Gospel sings the song that I've mentioned before, the shortest and most beautiful song in the world: "My God and my all." Look at one of the biggest problems in the world today; that is, the need to protect our earth, the natural resources that we have, along with all of the plants and animals and everything else that exists in this world. We are one with all of that; that's why Francis preached to the birds or St. Anthony of Padua spoke to the fish. That's why Francis was able to tame the wolf of Gubbio.

Some people say that the story of the wolf of Gubbio is really just a symbolic account of how Francis converted a robber named Lupo, which means "wolf." Well, maybe or maybe not, but it wouldn't surprise me if Francis did tame a wolf of Gubbio, as the story about him says. Again, Francis is so one with God that he's one with all creation. As a mystic, he was called to look deep into himself and recognize that he was brother and sister to everything God has made. And so who then is going to save the earth if not the mystics?

What about war? Look at wars that we have going on right now in the world; obviously, there are no easy solutions. We make this agreement, that agreement, and it all stops for awhile. But war will never really stop until we all recognize that we are brothers and sisters in God; until we reach out and accept other people, no matter how much they are like us or unlike us. Wars will end when we all do our part to bring real love into the world, which means that everyone really does get what belongs to them.

That may be a long time in coming. However long the human race has been able to have wars, they've had them. Wars have not ended in the two thousand years since Jesus's birth. But we don't give up; we keep saying this is not what God wants, and we keep working at peace.

Even Francis, with his perfect joy, had more of a life of hardship and trouble than a life of happy times. But in the end, he knows that his whole life has been given over to God, and he will be patient with the help God gives him. And he won't give up; he won't lose heart. That is part of the message Francis hands down to us.

It's not always easy to find the right thing to do; even when we do the loving thing, it doesn't necessarily change the situation right away. But again, I would say, don't give up; keep at it. This applies to many areas of our lives, and issues that are part of the world we live in. For example, what about capital punishment? What do I, as a person who is trying to live the Gospel, have to say about capital punishment? That brings up so many facets of what it is to live the Gospel, but again, we must keep asking ourselves that question in the hope that we will sense how God wants us to act.

Another area of concern is race relations and our feelings about people whose skin color is different from ours. A lot of people say, for instance, that the reason we have trouble with race relations is because we fear people who are different from us. Well, if I am one with God—my God and my all—how can I let that fear stay with me? I will learn to get beyond it.

What about developing countries? Some people there make maybe a hundred dollars a year, and they're trying to raise a family on that amount of money. Can we just let that go on? Aren't we called to do something about it? Maybe we can start by recognizing our own involvement in consumerism. How many clothes and electronic gadgets and tools and other such things do I buy in a year? Do I really need all that stuff? We can't change our habits and opinions overnight, but we can do something about it and get things moving in a more equitable direction.

We can't solve all the problems in the world; we're fortunate if we can deal with some of them and encourage other people who are doing something about them. We're used to hearing the general intercessions at Mass. During those intercessions we pray for different causes, different needs that are rampant in the world today, and we ask God to help these people. Through our intercessions, we will be praying for something that we want to do something about according to our circumstances. Maybe we can pray for the people who are hungry in Africa. We can't get on the next boat and take over a grocery cart full of food, but we can be aware of these people, be in tune with them, pray for them, pray for the people who are helping them.

What about the particular job you have? What if you are in health care, for instance, working as a doctor or a nurse? How would you as a human being help the people in your care? You find the right medicine as best you can and carry out all the procedures that are necessary for the health of that person, but maybe the most important thing is for you to care about the human being that is there. That may do as much or more for the health of that person than the particular procedures you might go through.

Francis helps us see that the way we save the world is to embrace it as God himself does. And we can do that not because we have the strength or even that we always have the exact know-how. We can do something for our world today and bring it more to God simply by being genuine in our relationship to him, and allowing his goodness to find its way through us. This is what we do want to do as followers of Francis, whether we are religious Franciscans, secular Franciscans, or Catholics or Christians in general—even people of no particular religious practice. This is the call we have.

Going back to the example I gave in the beginning of this chapter, of Ramakrishna, here is an Indian mystic who was faithful and genuine in his relationship to God. There are people all over the world and in all kinds of religions who are ready and able to do that as well. If we all say we will never give up but allow our religion to help us see who we really are—God's loving people—we will be able to make an impact on our world today. This is true whether we are talking about personal, social, or political arenas—any kind of activities we might be involved with.

We have the possibility to change the world and do our part; the world may not be what we want it to be when we die, but we might find that it has become a little bit better. And we will be able to pray, in spite of all the evidence against us, that it's still true: My God and my all.

A Little Bit about Secular Franciscans

What is a secular Franciscan? St. Francis established three different Orders. The first one is for the friars; the second is for nuns, such as the Poor Clares; and the third is for laypeople.

When Francis was establishing his Order, there were people who wanted to follow him but said, "We can't join your First Order, we have a different calling from God. We can't join the Second Order, we don't have that calling. How can we follow the Gospel as secular people?" Francis then gave them a Rule of their own to live by. Some people think that much of what Francis was calling people in his day to do is contained in the First Letter to All the Faithful, in which he invites the people to simply live the Gospel life. This means especially heeding the call of Christ to follow him and live the Beatitudes as best they can in their own particular way of life.

You might not know this, but Francis was not a priest himself; he really was a secular person. Although he did become a deacon, he was never a priest. The largest part of his life was spent as a secular person.

One of Francis's most important callings was that we go from Gospel to life and life to Gospel; that's what the Secular Franciscans are all about and what they try to incorporate and live throughout their life. By sharing in spiritual companionship through the larger fraternity groups of the Third Order, Secular Franciscans try to understand the Gospel as Francis did and then live it in their daily lives.

Secular Franciscans do not live the same way that people did in Francis's time, when the Order was established—nor do Franciscan friars or sisters, for that matter. But the focus of all Franciscan Orders is still the same as it was over eight hundred years ago in the time of Francis: to live the Gospel life in all that we do.

Personal Testimony from Two Secular Franciscans

BARBARA MULLIGAN

March of 1982 was a time of pain and sadness in my life. Yet it was also a time when the most exciting experience I've ever known happened to me: I met the Lord. I felt the overpowering love and presence of Jesus, and from that moment on, my life was changed. The pain and sadness were gone, replaced by a joy and strength I'd never known before.

I had read Scripture prior to this time, but after this experience with Jesus it was as though I'd never read a word of it before. It took on a whole new meaning. I knew that strength and perseverance come from the Lord, and nothing in the world could take that away. I intended to keep my eyes on Jesus.

As time passed, my hunger for Scripture increased. Since that time, my day is never complete if I don't read at least one passage from Scripture. Often times it will be more than that.

Shortly after my encounter with Jesus, God, in his infinite goodness, sent me a friend, my sister in Christ, Pauline. Our greatest common denominator was our desire to grow in our relationship with Jesus. We joined a Bible study class, started a prayer group of five people, and worked in parish ministry. But somehow that wasn't enough; something was missing.

One day, I was helping out with a class at the parish, and they showed a video of the life of St. Francis. I've been familiar with Francis all my life; he's the little man with a bird on his shoulder. There was only enough time to show half of St. Francis's life that day, and I was really disappointed; I couldn't wait to see the rest. Just as I'd seen Jesus so differently than ever before, I found the same thing was happening with Francis.

After Mass the next Sunday, a book in the parish book rack caught my eye: Murray Bodo's *Francis: The Journey and the Dream*. I bought it, and as I read it, I found what I had been searching for. Francis brought the Gospel to life. He carried out the commands of Jesus, literally. I was awed. I would never read the Good News again without thinking "Francis did that, Francis prayed that way, Francis told his brothers this or that." As all of this was unfolding, I thanked God and prayed that the Spirit would lead me in the next step.

As I was reading the Gospel of Luke one day, I felt that the Lord spoke to me through it. The passage is Luke 6:46–47: "Why do you call me 'Lord, Lord,' and do not do what I tell you? I will show you what someone is like who comes to me, hears my words, and acts on them." I began to think about times when

I might not have followed Christ in my daily life, and I found selfishness, prejudice, pride, many things I'd never seen before. This brought me to the sacrament of reconciliation, which I celebrated with a priest who understood and gave me guidance. I began to understand what the sacrament was all about.

After finishing *Francis: The Journey and the Dream*, I read three or four more books about the life of St. Francis and was more intrigued with the man than ever. Pauline was at the same point in her own spiritual journey, and we began talking about the Secular Franciscans. After prayer and discernment, we decided to look into the process of becoming one. I have never been sorry.

In the years since becoming a Secular Franciscan, I continue to learn the way of Francis. I shed much of the excess baggage I had carried through the earlier years of my life and simplified things immeasurably. I began to realize my needs were few, and I had far too much; possessions were no longer important. Internally, I continue to look into myself and my reaction to the people around me, and realize that I don't always react as Jesus would have.

As I strived to lead the Gospel life, it is not easy, but I know that by following in the footsteps of Francis, I am tracing a path straight to God.

PAULINE WILLIAMS

My initial conversion experience came at a time when I was in a very desperate situation. It came very simply. I was reading a book that had brief scriptural messages in it as daily guidance. I had read this book every day for two years before it had an impact on me. But one day, sitting alone in my dining room, the Lord touched me. I heard in my heart what this book was saying to me, instead of in my mind. That was the beginning of my search to become closer to Jesus.

In the months following that experience, I participated in a women's retreat, and saw Jesus so plainly in my sisters who attended that. That led me to my spiritual sharing and spiritual pal Barbara; I found Francis with her.

Throughout this time it was invaluable to attend meetings with other people, where we could all share stories about the difficulties in our life and how our faith was helping us to deal with these difficulties. These meetings helped me, as they did the others there, not to get discouraged in our pursuit of a closer relationship with Jesus.

Lately, I've been thinking a lot about why Jesus talks so much about lepers. When Francis first began his spiritual journey, he embraced a leper. This suggests that there is leper in all of us; we all have an opportunity to embrace the leper.

One final thing I'd like to mention. It has taken me many years to be able to see Jesus when I look in the mirror; being able to do this has brought me joy. I have learned that by letting Jesus into my heart and then out again, I can begin to see him in myself.

NOTES

1. See 1 Celano 82, in Marion A. Habig, ed., *Saint Francis of Assisi: Omnibus of Sources* (Cincinnati: Franciscan Media, 2008), p. 297. Cf. Bonaventure, Major Life, 10, 6, *Omnibus*, p. 710.
2. "Letter to a General Chapter," *Omnibus*, p. 107.
3. Bonaventure, "Major Life," 11, 1, *Omnibus*, p. 712.
4. Bonaventure, "Major Life," 11, 1, *Omnibus*, p. 712.
5. "The Rule of 1223," 1, *Omnibus*, p. 57.
6. Bonaventure, *Major Life*, 9, 22, *Omnibus*, p. 246.
7. "Legend of the Three Companions," 28–29, *Omnibus*, p. 917.
8. "Second Letter to All the Faithful," 3, in *Omnibus*, p. 92, citing John 6:64.
9. This prayer is adapted from the earliest words of St. Francis, dating from approximately 1205 when he was twenty-three years old. See Murray Bodo, *The Way of St. Francis: The Challenge of Franciscan Spirituality for Everyone* (Cincinnati: Franciscan Media, 1995), chapter five.
10. "Praises of God," *Omnibus*, p. 125.
11. *Omnibus*, p. 64.
12. Adapted from *Omnibus*, p. 77, citing John 14:6–9.
13. *Omnibus*, p. 93, citing John 6:64.
14. Adapted from *Omnibus*, p. 49.
15. "Early Rule," 22, *Omnibus*, p. 49.
16. "Admonition Seven," *Omnibus*, p. 81.
17. Adapted from "Admonition Eight," *Omnibus*, p. 82.
18. "Earlier Rule," 2, *Omnibus*, p. 32.
19. Bonaventure, "Major Life," 3, 3, *Omnibus*, p. 647.
20. Bonaventure, "Major Life," 1, 5, *Omnibus*, p. 639.
21. *Omnibus*, pp. 1448–1451.
22. *Omnibus*, p. 1448.
23. Adapted from *Omnibus*, p. 94.
24. See also *Francis and Clare: The Complete Works*, The Classics of Western Spirituality (Mahwah, N.J.: Paulist, 1982), p. 191.
25. *Omnibus*, p. 96.
26. *Omnibus*, p. 96.